I know someone like that

One man's search for normal in Norfolk

I know someone like that

Robert Ashton

turnpike farm
cultivating change

Turnpike Farm
Suton
Wymondham
NR18 9SS
www.turnpikefarm.co.uk
Tel: +44 (0)1953 605000

First published by Turnpike Farm in 2008

ISBN 978 0 95596 320 9

Printed and bound in Poland www.polskabook.pl
Copy editor and illustrations Alison Withers www.alisonwithers.co.uk
Layout, design and typesetting Graham Hales www.grahamhales.co.uk

LOTTERY FUNDED

rethink

This book was produced as part of the Moving People programme, funded by the
National Lottery through the Big Lottery Fund.

Contents

Foreword

A magnificent counterblast to the stigma and prejudice, ignorance and fear that afflicts the realm of mental health in this country,

I Know Someone Like That is a clear, readable and immensely touching account of how real people cope in the real world. I recommend this to everyone, for as the title suggests, we all know someone ...

Stephen Fry

Acknowledgements

This book marks my debut writing in a new genre. I am an established writer of books that guide the entrepreneur, but now I want to take you my reader on a different kind of journey. That journey would not have been possible without the help of some very dear people.

These include Jenny Manser, who first encouraged me to find myself. Sally Hart, a brilliant psychotherapist who helped along my own very personal journey a few years ago; Paul Corry of Rethink who wrote the bid that won the funding to make the book possible; Anne Smales my super PA who arranged most of the interviews; each of my interviewees who were brave enough to tell their stories and agree to see them published; Alison Withers who edited and challenged the copy, as well as doing the illustrations; Stephen Fry who took the project seriously and was impressed enough to write a kind foreword and finally my wife Belinda, who has supported me every step of the way and without whom I would have achieved nothing.

Finally, let me acknowledge your role as reader. If this book helps you see the people around with more understanding, then it has done its job. But the book alone can change nothing. It needs you and I thank you in advance for the difference you will make having read it.

Introduction

Every living person on this planet has prejudices. They are the product of culture, circumstance and the pressure to conform that each and every one of us feels. Prejudice is natural and helps us create boundaries. The alternative is to be overwhelmed with choice!

Prejudices are usually expressed as preferences: the way we choose to behave and interact with our neighbours. I, for example, would prefer my daughter not to marry a boy with ginger hair. You'll understand that this is not a matter I am able to influence, but it is my preference all the same.

My reasons are largely irrational. I would like to have grandchildren that tan easily and don't spend their lives hiding from the sun. This preference is based on my own childhood experience of playing outside, going brown and taking pleasure from feeling the warm sun on my bare back. If my daughter moved a thousand miles North, this opportunity for outdoor play would not present itself often enough for my 'yet to be born' grandchildren to play in the sun.

Take my preference to its logical extreme and my daughter might also choose to have children with a man of African descent. Indeed she works in a field where visits to Africa are probable, rather than possible. How would I feel if she fell for a man from Equatorial Africa? My grandchildren in this instance would be far better able than me to enjoy the sun without fear of burning. Would this give me a problem too?

Mixed race children face other challenges. They can feel that they are neither of one race or the other. Playground taunts can make them feel somehow different and rejected. This can increase their susceptibility to mental ill health. Marginalisation can make us ill.

What started out as a minor prejudice against ginger hair becomes more complex when I am presented with the other extreme; coffee coloured grandchildren. When forced to make a choice and decide which option I consider the 'lesser of two evils' I begin to feel distinctly uncomfortable.

Luckily I also know that I'll have no say in the matter. Whilst my daughter might well ask for my opinion, she is strong minded enough to follow her own instinct and do what she feels is right for her. That means I might have to visit some of my prejudices and, moreover, change them!

And it's always been this way. We have an inbuilt, almost unconscious, ability to isolate and shun anyone who fails to match our perception of normality. It is a basic animal instinct. If a cow in a field becomes ill, the others will move away and graze somewhere else. If someone starts behaving strangely in the street, we behave in exactly the same way; we move away, suspicious and uncomfortable.

It could be argued then that prejudice is a fundamental defence mechanism that for at least the last few thousand years has been past its 'sell by date'.

Prejudice survives, perhaps even thrives, in the world today because we're mostly too busy with our day-to-day lives to unpick the complex feelings that underlie them. With the world's population at an all time high, we also have the luxury of choice. We can live a full and active life without spending time with those our prejudices encourage us to avoid.

We do this at work as well as in a social context. Despite comprehensive legislation to protect the rights of minority groups, employers still allow personal prejudice to influence their recruitment processes. People with health problems, disabilities or even a different sexual orientation are somehow less successful when they apply for a job.

Workplace discrimination works both ways. Gay employers often feel more comfortable with gay employees. Young employers will avoid hiring older workers. An Asian entrepreneur will be more inclined to recruit other Asians than equally qualified white people. Of course we all know that actually, people should recruit on ability alone. But every group naturally feels more comfortable with people who fit in and won't seem out of place.

The purpose of this book is to illustrate the folly of prejudice. The interviews it contains each explore one life and the impact prejudice has had upon it. What unites the people featured is that at the time of interview, they lived in Norfolk. As such they share the same space, see the same local TV shows and perhaps even shop in the same supermarket.

You could be forgiven for thinking that Norfolk is somewhat monocultural with everyone sharing the same views. If you did, you would be wrong. There are people from every corner of the globe quietly living in Norfolk. There are people who have survived holocausts, economic migrants and people born locally who consider themselves very different from their neighbours.

There is no such thing as "normal" for Norfolk!

This book was funded by the Big Lottery Fund as part of a major mental health anti-stigma campaign delivered by mental health charities Rethink, Mind and Mental Health Media. You may wonder why this introduction only now mentions mental health. The fact is that mental illness is in many cases simply a symptom of a deeper issue. Put simply, being the victim of prejudice can damage your mental health.

Mental illness can be caused by changes in the brain chemistry, or exposure to prolonged physical or emotional discomfort. There are many causes and even more diagnoses. Our susceptibility to mental illness lies hidden beneath the surface. It often needs external factors to cause sufficient distress or discomfort to turn a hidden vulnerability into a full-blown mental health condition.

It is not enough, then, to challenge the many and varied prejudices that create the stigma experienced by people with mental health problems. What's needed is deeper than that.

This book can do no more than illustrate by example how we are all very different and that difference enriches, rather than threatens, our very existence.

Each person interviewed for this book has either experienced prejudice or perhaps unwittingly imposed it. Each person interviewed is entitled to their views and opinions and I as narrator have tried hard to remain impartial. Of course I have prejudices too. Indeed I started by sharing one of them.

The process of writing this book has forced me to take a fresh look at how I view the people around me. I hope reading it does the same for you.

Robert Ashton

One

Appearances are deceptive

'You see, but do not observe'

Sir Arthur Conan Doyle

Adventures of Sherlock Holmes (1892)

You don't need to be a detective to know that we can all be very quick to form a first opinion. We meet new people and rapidly make all kinds of assumptions about them from the way they look, dress or behave.

Yet appearances can be deceptive and frequently are. As Sherlock Holmes pointed out to his assistant Dr Watson, you have to observe as well as see. Otherwise your understanding of the people you meet never goes beyond that first impression gained in an initial glance.

This point was brought home to me in a very real way several years ago. For my 40th birthday, I treated myself to bus driving lessons and passed the PCV test. Occasionally, just for fun, I would drive coach loads of usually older people on various excursions. I would be wearing a shirt and tie that bore the logo of the company whose coach I was driving.

It soon became very obvious that because I was in the driver's seat for them, they automatically assumed that I drove coaches every day. Of course that was not a silly thing to assume as most coach drivers do drive for a living and not, as I did, for fun. From what they said to me it was obvious they assumed that I was earning a low wage, 'working class' in my outlook and in some ways a victim as driving a coach is not a glamorous job.

Had they spotted the laptop I took with me so that I could write whilst they were visiting whatever attraction formed the day's destination, they might have questioned me and found out more about my motivation for being their driver for the day. None ever did and in some ways that's a shame.

Looking different

Can you imagine being told you're so ugly you have to walk around with a bag over your head? Think what it would do for your self esteem. Imagine if it was your mother who had decided this and chosen to keep you hidden away because she thought other kids would laugh at you. You'd probably hate yourself and wonder why you'd even been born.

In his 2007 film 'The Orphanage', Spanish film director, Juan Antonio Bayona, has cast his play out of that scenario with disastrous consequences. The mother works at an orphanage, and makes her disfigured son wear a sack over his head when he plays with the orphans.

The kids all go to play in a cave on the beach one afternoon. Being kids, they pull off and hide the poor boy's mask. He refuses to leave the darkness of the cave without it and drowns when the tide comes in. His mother takes her revenge by killing the children.

It's a dark and sinister story, but one that illustrates well the folly of stigma. In this case, the stigma is brought on to her son by the mother. She thinks he's ugly, she thinks he'll be teased and by placing a bag over his head, she brings about the very situation she was seeking to avoid.

Of course it's only a story. But is real life so different? Kids can be cruel, and parents will always do what they can to protect their offspring. Sometimes, however, the effort to protect is misplaced. What would have happened if the mother had told her son he was uniquely beautiful? What if she had told him to ignore the glances and looks, because they were the result of envy and not disgust? The story would then have had a very different ending.

Real life is no different from fiction. Real parents impose their prejudices and fears onto their offspring, yet times and attitudes change. Or do they?

Kelly

Like most 29 year olds, Kelly is not looking forward to her 30th birthday. It's one of those big milestones in your life that few meet with enthusiasm. What makes it special for Kelly, though, is that for a time she didn't think she'd live long enough to celebrate the big day.

At the age of 15, Kelly was diagnosed with brain cancer. The tumour was in a place where it could not be reached by surgeons, so she had to endure years of chemo and radio therapy. All this coincided with her time at sixth form. Despite her illness and the debilitating effect of treatment, she kept going to school and, to her credit, passed the course.

Teenage girls are very image conscious and Kelly was no exception. Her waist-length brown hair fell out almost as soon as her treatment started. The idea of a wig was far from appealing and so she decided to be bold and bald.

Being bold and proudly displaying what many would consider as a visual handicap is a brave move. She was encouraged by her parents to be 'out' about her illness and not to try to hide it away. This was as courageous for them as it was for her; I'm sure they didn't enjoy the prospect of people seeing their daughter without hair. Equally, the very real possibility that they would lose her altogether must have put the decision into context.

So was Kelly exposed to prejudice and stigma? Not nearly as much as if she'd chosen to wear a wig, she told me. 'Wigs are what people use to hide something,' she said, going on to emphasise that she had nothing at all to feel ashamed about.

Strangely she had no problem with the boys on her course. They were mostly sympathetic and kind. Girls, however, were not always quite so kind. There was one incident she remembers vividly that involved being asked to comment on styles in a hair magazine. Not something she really wanted to do! 'It was either very unthinking or a deliberate dig at my baldness,' she said.

Wisely, she kept the hair that fell out and today wears some of it as hair extensions in what little hair she has grown since her recovery. Her oncologist told her it would never re-grow and apart from some down, he was right. However, she can rightly say that the shoulder-length hair she now sports is her own.

You might dismiss Kelly's response to being shown a hair magazine as simply being over sensitive. After all, she was being treated for cancer and that's bound to make you touchy.

But think again.

This was not a tactless gesture made without thought and quickly followed by an apology. It was a deliberate move to emphasise to Kelly and her circle of friends that Kelly looked different and therefore was somehow no longer the same; no longer one of the group. Although the intention to push her out of the group was perhaps not a conscious one, it was there all the same.

Looking older

In our culture we can be very suspicious of any relationship between two people with widely differing ages. Although within the family, the value of grandparents in childrearing is widely recognised, an older person befriending an unrelated child is viewed with great suspicion.

When you reach adulthood, it becomes acceptable and even fashionable to have a mentor; someone older and wiser to help you pick your way through life's minefield. In many work situations, mentoring is actively encouraged and arranged. Organisations such as the Prince's Trust recruit and train mentors to help young people from disadvantaged backgrounds succeed in self-employment.

Management writer Charles Handy talks of the importance of what he terms 'golden seeds'. These are nuggets of self confidence, given to a young person by someone unrelated. That person tells them that they are capable of reaching their seemingly unattainable goal. Spurred on by this unbiased encouragement, the golden seed sown, they go on to do great things.

Yet despite the obvious potential value of mentoring and encouragement we are generally quick to make the wrong assumptions.

Not everyone who befriends someone of a different generation has a sinister motive. But we let the fear of the minority prevent the majority from benefiting from a wider network of friends and supporters.

Sex is usually the fear, with age differences deemed to be the likely cause of inequality of power, domination and even exploitation. After all, how would you feel if your 19 year-old undergraduate son started dating a woman of 37? And what if they married? How would you feel then?

Heather and Neville

I met Heather and her husband Neville soon after they moved to Norfolk. They found that by selling a large house in Lincoln and buying a more modest place here, Neville

22

could afford to retire early. Waiting until he was 65 and able to draw his full local authority pension would have shortened the time they could spend together. Neville is 18 years younger than Heather. (When I met them, Neville was 59 and Heather 77).

They met when Neville was a 19 year-old student and Heather the 37 year-old manager of his college canteen. The age gap was accentuated by world events; Heather can well remember the air raids, rationing and other deprivations of World War Two Britain. Those wartime memories, many happy, some tinged with sadness, are hers alone for her husband of some 37 years was born after the war had ended.

'We had very different childhoods,' she told me, 'yet now we see the world in exactly the same way.' Although they do not wear matching clothes, it is fair to say that the couple are close. See them together and the non-verbal communication is almost telepathic. Each is aware of the points at which the other is likely to want to enter the conversation.

After college, Heather embarked on a career in catering. She enjoyed the work and was good at it. Promotion came quickly and by her mid thirties she found herself managing the catering at a teacher training college in Oxford. Largely because of the long, unsocial hours she was working, she also found herself still single; it did not feel like a problem.

Love arrived in the form of a young student teacher who immediately caught her eye. He was handsome, bright and not yet twenty. Her first instinct was to shun his affections simply because he was so young. 'I thought he'd grow out of it and find a girl his own age', she commented, glancing across the room at her husband. As we know, he did not!

Heather is from a generation that listened to their mothers. In fact, so is her husband and it was his mother who, as the relationship blossomed, had the gravest doubts. 'My mother thought he was wonderful,' she said, 'but his mother was less certain.' Gentle probing reveals that, as with many mothers of boys, Neville's mother was very discerning when it came to his choice of replacement for her in his affections. There is perhaps always a difference here between sons and mothers and daughters and mothers.

'I was more worried about the balance of power,' explained Heather. 'I had savings and a well paid job. Neville had very little because he had not yet started his career'. She went on to explain that even in the swinging sixties tradi- tional thinking dictated that when a couple married, the man should support the woman and not the other way around.

In fact, it was also parental control that led to Heather meeting her husband. When she graduated she had wanted to emigrate to New Zealand. Her father, however, did not share her enthusiasm for such a large step and told her she was not to go. Would a recently graduated daughter be so obedient today, I wonder? Or indeed, would a father be so keen to influence the direction of his daughter's career? Probably not.

Both agreed that in their day, parents were only too keen to project their ambitions onto their young. Most parents aspired to see their children do better than them. Not a lot better, but just enough to make them more secure, more content and free from poverty. A good job was in those days a job for life and people were discouraged from moving around. Promotion was achieved as often as not by stepping into 'dead man's shoes'. To push yourself forward was frowned upon. Progress was as much the product of good fortune as it was of skill and ability.

Having a much younger husband has certainly kept Heather young, both in appearance and outlook. Despite being in her mid seventies she has no grey hair and assured me she did not colour it. The couple's friends tend to be aged somewhere between the two of them and clearly the age gap has never posed a problem.

Her husband Neville admitted that as a young man he had preferred the company of older people and so was content to find his circle of contacts now largely his age or older. In fact he appears to be young for his age as well; he most certainly is not a 'pipe and slippers' man!

As you would expect, the couple have experienced some gentle ribbing over the years but are very much immune to it now. Neville worked in the public sector before retiring and for a while had a role that involved reducing stigma. His marriage is a clear illustration of the importance of giving people the credit for knowing what is right for them. The couple's philosophy is very much to treat people as people and accept them for what they are, not what your prejudices might suggest they might or ought to be.

The couple did not have children and so have always had time to do things together, free of distraction. 'It's not that we didn't want any,' Heather said, 'more that it just didn't happen for us.' That said, they do share a large number of nephews and nieces and so are in many ways surrogate grandparents. They most certainly are not lonely and lead as active a life as they ever have. I wonder what their mothers would think of the relationship if they were alive today?

It's difficult to know how to reduce these very natural fears in parents. The problem is that they rarely live long enough to celebrate their child's 40th wedding anniversary. Perhaps the answer is to put more faith in young people to know their minds and make rational decisions.

Acting strangely

We are very quick to stereotype people. It's how we make sense of the sheer volume of folk we meet in the course of our everyday life. Remember that until a couple of hundred years ago you'd rarely meet anyone you didn't know. We all lived in small, self-contained, largely rural communities where everyone knew everyone. That's not to say that our 19th century ancestors were not challenged by people who seemed very different. Evangelists, tinkers, storytellers, soldiers and people from the continent and further afield would visit the remotest of places from time to time. They often stood out from the crowd, but at least people knew everyone in the crowd!

Stereotyping makes it possible for us to group the people we encounter and avoid being overwhelmed by them. It enables us to make rapid assessments; is this person a threat or an opportunity? What do they want from me? Do I even want them to notice me? These and other questions ricochet around our minds, often sub-consciously. What's more they lead us into all kinds of traps.

An example very personal to me concerns diabetes. My wife of 25 years has been insulin dependent since she was a toddler. She constantly has to balance her diet with her insulin injections. If she gets it wrong, she can easily become hypoglycaemic. Low blood sugar makes you unsteady on your feet, can slur your speech and make you generally disorientated. It's rather like being drunk!

So imagine how people respond if on a shopping trip her blood sugar falls dangerously low. People's first reaction is not always to offer help but to scorn her for being drunk in the city centre in the middle of the day. It's a reasonable assumption to make - but totally incorrect.

People who live with poor mental health can also behave strangely. I interviewed several for this book and not all were willing for me to share their experiences. One man in particular was adamant that mankind was close to destruction. He felt he had been forewarned by some greater being and that he, and a few other believers, would be spared the apocalypse into which the rest of us are, in his mind, about to tumble.

'I know that this is the Truth' he told me, stressing the importance of the capital T in the word Truth. As interviewer and author of this book, I could not have an opinion (although I rather hope he's proved wrong!). Instead I wrote up our interview sensitively and without bias. Everyone is entitled to their view after all. My refusal to accept what I saw as his view as fact meant that he withdrew permission to be featured in this book.

My point is this. To each and every one of us, our perceptions of the world and each other are reality. Our perceptions shape our behaviour and actions, as surely as do hunger and sexual desire. Christians amongst you will be reminded of the story of Noah. He decided to build an ark when those around him were confident the floods he forecast would not come. In the story we're told how he was actually proved right.

None of us has the ability to build an ark in our mind when it's already being flooded by prejudice. It's too late and we drown in a sea of inequality we have created ourselves. It's better to give people the benefit of the doubt; to tolerate their different views, appearances and behaviours. The laws of the land allow for great diversity of opinion and action. Let's embrace them!

Want to look closer at the way we see and judge each other? Here are three things you might try:

Talk to people you don't know – encourage people to tell you about themselves and compare what they say with your existing perceptions of them. Be prepared to be surprised. Start a conversation on the bus, in the pub or on the street.

Look back and then reflect forward – history is littered with examples of how people misjudged others by appearance, age, or behaviour. Who, of the people you know and respect today, might have in a former time have been confined to jail or the workhouse? (British gays and single mothers at one time endured this treatment)

Research how other cultures define normal behaviour and discuss with your friends how you feel about these differences. Explore why you feel they are good or bad. Form a considered opinion on issues that impact on our increasingly diverse society. Topics to consider might include the age of sexual consent, democracy versus dictatorship in turbulent regions, arranged marriages, euthanasia.

Two

Me myself I

'I am the captain of my soul'

William Henley
Invictus (1875)

One thing that differentiates mankind from every other living creature is our strong sense of self. From an early age we can recognise ourselves in a mirror, something your pet dog or cat is simply not bright enough to do. We can also remember things in great detail as well as think forward, anticipate, expect.

We grow up knowing what we are, remembering where we've been and often with a strong sense of where we want to go. Yet we are too often encouraged to put not ourselves but others first. In fact history is littered with examples of societies where people were expected to conform, to sacrifice self in the pursuit of what was presented as the common good.

Psychologists no doubt have clever ways to describe this phenomenon. To me as a writer, it is far simpler. I only need to think back to the First World War to realise how our Western European culture created in a generation of young men, British, German and many others, a willingness to volunteer for almost certain death.

The story of Rudyard Kipling's only son captures the tragedy of this behaviour for me perfectly. Young Jack Kipling was helped by his father to bypass the medical rules, only to die in a crater when he lost his glasses and could not see his way to escape. Who killed him in reality? The German who fired the fatal shell or the father who persuaded him to volunteer? For me the jury is still out on that one.

I have to say that as a parent, I find it difficult to imagine any situation that would lead me to encourage my child to risk death in such a way. Was Kipling's love of his country greater than that for his son? Did he not realise that in ten years' time the war would be nothing more than history; that in ten years' time his son would still be a young man facing a long, happy life? Perhaps I'm missing a point, or perhaps I'm not!

Being yourself

As I look around today I see people who are doing what they believe others expect of them; expected by society, expected by parents, partner, boss or child. It can be very convenient to dedicate your life to doing what you think other people think you should do. It avoids the need to make decisions for yourself!

Failing to set your own life agenda can be very damaging. As time goes by you can become increasingly frustrated as you acquire more and more duty and move further and further from doing what you want. The stress of this lifestyle can damage your mental health.

Paradoxically, the mental health of someone you love can actually be the precursor to a dramatic life change. People with very poor mental health can be very demanding and need a lot of care. Across the world there are literally millions of people, often mothers, who dedicate their life to helping their unwell adult child cope.

Equally, there are people whose lives are touched by mental illness in some way who then decide to get involved. They give up their careers and re-train to work in this fascinating and challenging field. It's a world where your heart is as important as your head. It's a world where you feel as well as think. It's a world that delivers, for many people, true self actualisation; the chance to do something they feel passionately about.

Tony

A quietly-spoken Norfolk man, Tony is 55 and lives in a rural village with his son. In mid life he gave up his career and retrained as a mental health worker. He spends his time in schools, helping young people understand mental illness. His mission is to reduce stigma. 'People in Norfolk can have a very narrow viewpoint,' he told me. 'They simply don't understand'.

Tony on the other hand understands only too well. He married young and when their son was born, his wife suffered from post-natal depression. 'She just couldn't settle,' he said, as he described to me the way their idyllic life was gradually and steadily eroded by his wife's declining mental health.

She did not respond to treatment and was diagnosed schizophrenic. He became unable to provide the level of care she needed as well as raise their son and hold down a full-time job. Their relationship fell apart and she went into specialist residential care. Later, she died, tragically young.

When his son reached the age of 20 he too became ill. The doctors diagnosed paranoid psychosis and Tony now finds himself caring for him. His son has a job, but lives with his father and is unlikely to easily make the transition to independent living.

Not surprisingly, these intense, personal experiences have prompted strong feelings in Tony. He has witnessed prejudice, stigma and ignorance first hand. He has also seen the two people he loved the most taken apart by mental illness.

It would not have surprised anyone if Tony had himself succumbed to the pressure and become ill. Instead he decided to spend the rest of his life working to change attitudes towards mental illness.

'The best sessions I run are those where a service user tells their story,' he said as he described the work he does with schools. 'Young people are quick to spot that someone with poor mental health is a human being with a problem, not a problem human being!'

Through his new career he has met and fallen for a new partner. He calls her his girlfriend as, although they've been together for 20yrs, they choose to live independently. She has a daughter living with bi-polar disorder and he has his son. Thankfully they also now have each other.

Tony's experience is not as unusual as you might think. Many people who work in the mental health field were prompted to do so by personal experience. Sometimes it is their own health that has been poor. When they recover it often seems like a natural step to help others making that same journey. It's the same motivation that makes people who found school stimulating become teachers, or people who discovered physical fitness to become personal trainers.

James

Despite being only 23 years old, James has worked as a freelance personal trainer for almost three years. Before that he worked at a local gym, developing the skills and qualifications he needed. When he started his own business several gym members became his first clients. Several of those, me included, still rely on him to give them the training and motivation to get fit and look good.

James, however, did not always look good. As a child he ate too much of the wrong foods and became overweight (he describes himself as having been a 'fat kid'). In common with many overweight children he was badly teased at school and did not enjoy his time there. Again, in common with many who find themselves the victims of bullying, he ate more, taking comfort from his food. This did not help him to gain a more socially acceptable physique.

Then one day something changed. He has never told me what it was that tipped him into action, but something did. He started to exercise and take account of what he ate and drank. He worked out, ate sensibly and in his own way fought back against those who made fun of him. His mission as a personal trainer is to support other people as they make their own physical transformations. Not surprisingly he is very good at his job and very much in demand. There are a lot of personal trainers out there now, although few have James' passion and drive.

Losing weight, getting fit and working for himself have made James unusually independent, confident and mature for his age. He now lives with his fiancée and is about as far from being a quiet, 'fat kid' as is possible.

It is nearly always some life event, trauma or experience that prompts us to make significant changes to our lives. Often that experience is brought about by the actions of others. When confronted by prejudice and stigma we either submit and suffer or fight back in some way or the other.

It's never too late

No matter how old you are, you always have some life ahead of you. You cannot predict, unless terminally ill, when you are most likely to die. We all assume and hope that we will live to be really old and indeed, most of us do!

Delia

I'm sure Delia will forgive me for sharing her age with you. She is in her 60s. Life has not been overly kind to her either. She's had three children, never been particularly well off and suffered from breast cancer around eight years ago. Luckily this was successfully treated, but the fact remains that Delia has not had an easy life.

I don't mean to be unkind, more to make the point that she is not some glamorous granny with stunning good looks and life's odds stacked in her favour. Delia is like so many women her age; she has lived every year of her life.

Inside, though, Delia is nowhere near her age. In fact in my view, she is probably getting younger every year. The reason is simple; Delia is now following her true vocation and not simply working to make a living.

It was not always so easy to discover and follow a dream. Delia, in common with many of her generation did as she was told. Her parents believed in private education and Delia was their third child to go to an independent school. (She also had twin sisters and a brother following in her foot-steps!)

Although bright, Delia found academic work difficult. She eventually found out she was slightly dyslexic. 'That explains why I was so good at maths and not so good at English,' she sighed. She only got two 'O' Levels and felt a failure. That feeling of being in what she calls 'the second league' remained with her for decades, dogging her career and holding her back.

Ambitions came and went. 'I wanted to be a games teacher, but wasn't good enough at sport,' she told me.

Already naturally shy, Delia's self confidence was not improved by these rejections. Her father suggested languages and Delia went abroad to learn Spanish, German and French all at the same time. One year later she passed 'A' Level French, surely a considerable achievement for someone later found to be dyslexic!

'These exam results helped me to see that I was as able as anyone else,' Delia told me. 'I knew then that if I applied myself I could succeed. My challenge was to find the motivation I had lacked throughout my schooling'.

By her own admission, Delia drifted through the next few years. Friends who were teachers encouraged her to try for teacher training college. She followed their advice and became a teacher. 'I knew the subjects', she explained, 'but was too shy to be really good in the classroom.'

Delia married and had three children herself and this meant taking a number of career breaks. However, it was when her children were safely established in their own careers and she and her husband had both retired that she gained the confidence to follow her heart and be the person she had perhaps always wanted to be.

Delia had spasmodically attended church all her life. She had been regularly attending her local Methodist church of late. She'd found her faith had helped her cope with a number of family issues over the years; none serious, but all worrying just the same.

Now, at an age when most people are content to retire, she is training to be a Methodist Lay preacher. Her faith has become stronger and she's began taking an active role in the life of her church. 'It was just like when I decided to train to be a teacher,' she said. 'It took the encouragement of friends I could trust to take the plunge and do it.'

Today Delia is being herself, perhaps for the first time in her life. She is doing something she believes in, enjoys and knows helps others as well as herself. Delia still looks her age, but she acts much, much younger. Being herself has made her cheerful, energetic and enthusiastic. She literally radiates happiness. Could she have done this years ago if her parents and peers had been more encouraging? Of course she could; Delia did what was expected of her for a lifetime before taking control and following her heart.

Becoming someone else

For most of us, being "me" is about having the freedom to be oneself. It sounds simple, but in our complex world, it can actually be very difficult to unlearn those obedient behaviours and explore your real purpose. It is never too late and rarely wrong to follow your instinct and be yourself.

Personal change almost inevitably attracts attention; not all of it welcome. That's why it's so important for us all to become more tolerant and understanding. Some people make changes to their lives that can really challenge our self perception. An example is when someone decides that they have one gender and occupy the body of another.

Gender change is perhaps one of the most traumatic experiences someone can endure in their quest to be comfortable in their skin. The experts on sexuality tell us that very few of us are 100% one thing or the other, in our minds at least. Physical gender is determined at conception; sexuality is far more complex and far less straightforward.

Kerry

Kerry's bungalow resembles a fortress. Semi-detached, unprepossessing and overlooking open farmland, you enter without Kerry's consent at your peril. Behind a large fence live two very large dogs. The roadside windows are of armoured glass and CCTV cameras capture a record of all who venture up the drive. Kerry feels threatened.

In fact threats and rejection have dominated Kerry's life. Born in 1944, the product of a fleeting union between an airman and a local girl she was put up for adop- 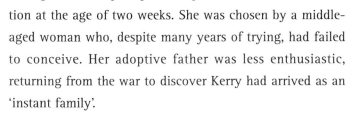 tion at the age of two weeks. She was chosen by a middle-aged woman who, despite many years of trying, had failed to conceive. Her adoptive father was less enthusiastic, returning from the war to discover Kerry had arrived as an 'instant family'.

At the age of five, she was despatched to an all-boys' boarding school, where, already insecure, she was quickly to fall prey to bullies. 'Although I was a boy then, I somehow felt different', she told me. 'They were not happy years.'

It was only in her early teens that she found someone who took an interest in her and offered her encouragement. Kerry remembers him well, although not fondly. On a bright yellow counterpane he subjected her to appalling abuse. 'His was the first erection I ever saw', she said, grimacing at the memory. 'He was also the first man I saw ejaculate.'

Confused further by these adolescent experiences, Kerry sought to prove her masculinity. She developed a passion for outdoor pursuits and, living at this time on the Isle of Wight, swam and fished at every opportunity.

Her first job was at a trout fishery in the Lincolnshire Wolds although she did not stay there long. Damaged by her past she felt the need to keep moving on. The anonymity of London appealed to her and she found a job in a West End gun shop. After a promising start, she was offered an apprenticeship, but with that came responsibility and that proved to be too much for her.

Despite what she describes as 'continuing undercurrents of doubt' she married at 21, although it was only two years later that the marriage was fully consummated. That relationship lasted nine years and produced a daughter from whom she is currently estranged.

During this time she joined the fire service and being tall, fit and strong found the work enjoyable as well as challenging. 'As a fireman you see some distressing sights, help people in a time of need and win the admiration of many,' she commented. 'What no one knew was that underneath the uniform, I was becoming increasingly distressed myself'.

Her second wife was 'recruited' through a dating agency. They married after just six weeks, not long enough for Kerry to realise she was marrying an alcoholic. That relationship also ended in tears.

It was Kerry's third wife who introduced her to Norfolk. A son from a previous relationship lived in the county and they moved to both be closer to him and because property prices were such that they could afford a nice house with land. Kerry wanted a smallholding, perhaps to nurture that love of the outdoors that developed during her troubled adolescence. After yet another acrimonious divorce Kerry decided to stay in Norfolk and purchased the bungalow in which she lives today.

It was a combination of factors that led Kerry to become a woman. Uncomfortable with both hetero and homosexual sex, she knew something was wrong, but could not find an answer. She had worked in one of the most macho environments, yet this had not made her feel any more content as a man. She had also endured mental ill health, which at one time required in-patient care at a psychiatric hospital.

It was her local GP who found the key that unlocked her gender conundrum. Referring her to a psychiatrist enabled her to fully explore her feelings for the first time. Specialist support was found at the Charing Cross Hospital, a centre for trans-gender work, and at last Kerry began to see a future.

The journey from man to woman is long and arduous. Careful counselling enables you to explore every aspect of your gender, sexuality and identity. Hormone treatment, together with a requirement to live as a woman for two full years before surgery can be considered, put Kerry under intense pressure. Her then employer found it all too much and she had to seek a new job, out of the public gaze. (She now works a late shift cleaning buses.)

'My journey has taught me a lot about people,' she exclaimed, 'because while some friends have vanished, others emerged, often from quite surprising quarters.' One of her most supportive friends is her ex wife who now describes her as her 'big sister'. Another is a half brother she only found out existed a few years ago.

Kerry makes friends with some difficulty. The memory of childhood abuse by a man she came to trust has left her reluctant to trust and suspicious of all who take an interest in her. This to some extent explains the fortifications that make her bungalow feel safe.

Paradoxically, she needs good friends now more than ever. Living as a woman and facing radical surgery, she has to learn a lifetime's worth of femininity. She now has breasts, but finds buying a bra difficult. Make-up, clothing and mannerisms all need to be learned. After years of feeling deep down she is a woman, now she has to learn to be a woman, naturally and without attracting attention.

Not surprisingly, she attracts more than a casual glance from people who pass her in the street. She is after all more than six foot tall and has a somewhat rugged face for a woman. However life is becoming increasingly sweet as, despite the stigma and stares, she grows in confidence as the woman she so clearly has become.

For Kerry, that struggle to find herself; the quest to be 'me', has taken a lifetime of confusion to unravel. When you read this book, she will have had her surgery and at last, be a woman in both body and mind.

As we mature as individuals, we learn to compromise. To balance the natural desire to be ourselves, with the need to be what others expect us to be. It seems, though, that as we get older we compromise less and sometimes go to great lengths to become the person we feel we really are.

Others, like James, are lucky enough to be prompted at an early age to shake off the negative aspects of their persona and take control. Some seem to give up and spend their lives serving others and neglecting themselves.

We all have a responsibility to encourage and support those around us in their search for themselves.

To what extent are you the person you want to be? Here are three things you might think about or discuss with those around you:

Make time to find yourself – many people go on retreat to spend time alone with themselves; start with an afternoon on the beach or in the park. Get outdoors and think about your life and where it's heading

Explore your prejudices – we all pick up prejudice and bias from others. Parents, for example, raise us with their views. Times change though. Discuss how things are different today and what this means. Do you need to take a fresh look at your prejudices?

Ask your friends to describe you – this is a great group exercise and enables you to discover how others see you. It can be great fun if not taken too seriously. You can learn a lot about yourself by listening to others describing you.

Three

Belonging

'Home sweet home; there's no place like home'

John Payne

'Clari, the Maid of Milan' (1822) An opera

It is perhaps ironic that the man who wrote the famous song, 'Home Sweet Home' did so when he was thousands of miles from his birthplace. He was probably homesick! John Payne was a New Yorker but came to Britain as a young man and made his career as an actor and writer. Today, New York is simply a seven hour flight from London. In the early 19th century crossing the Atlantic took 20 or more days.

If you were lucky enough to have been born into a happy, loving family, then you will have fond memories of your childhood home. It's the place you felt safe, free from danger and oblivious to many of the realities of life. You were fed when hungry, cleaned when dirty and comforted when afraid.

As you grow older and more independent, you venture further from home; forging new, trusting relationships with people you call friends. Then in adulthood, you create a home of your own, where perhaps you raise children of your own.

For me, home is more than just my physical refuge from the world. It extends beyond the physical into the emotional space I choose to occupy. I guess you'd call this my comfort zone. This wider home includes the activities I regularly enjoy, the people I regularly meet and the work I regularly undertake. It's very the space I occupy with my life. Others will have their own safe space, which might have very different dimensions from my own.

One thing that everyone's home space will contain is other people. It's difficult to enjoy life on your own; we need to feel we belong, are wanted and respected. We are communal creatures and mostly happiest in a circle of people we know and trust.

Home, then, can be a place in your head as well as a place you rest your head.

Moving home

Many people are unhappy about the wave after wave of economic migrants that are hitting our country. Even in a rural county like Norfolk, you can't fail to notice the Eastern European accents you seem to hear everywhere.

Economic migration is not new. People have been moving to Norfolk for centuries; from Flemish Huguenots in the 17th century to Polish airmen who opted to stay here after the Second World War. Today, a city such as Norwich might look white British, but in reality it contains people born in just about every country in the world. The fact that you don't notice them is perhaps a testimony to the extent to which the city welcomes, embraces and adopts them.

Sometimes, though, the experience of those moving here is at odds with our expectations. They can actually feel isolated by bureaucracy's attempts to make them feel at home.

Georgetta

Georgetta was born in Bucharest. Her father, a Croatian, was a specialist engineer working for one of the biggest hydro-electric stations in Romania. Her mother was half Polish, half Russian, but both parents considered themselves Romanian. Her grandfather joined the Communist Party in the 1920s, albeit briefly, and as a family they accepted as normal the way things were in Eastern Europe. She grew up with the Cold War in a country with recently-changed boundaries. She describes Romania as a Latin island surrounded by a Slavic sea.

Languages have always been important to Georgetta, and like most Romanian children she started learning foreign languages before school age. At school, two languages were mandatory and she became proficient in English and French. This was an era when travel outside the Eastern Bloc was illegal except for the privileged few; they were usually only allowed to go if someone close to them remained at home. Defection was rarely possible and always painful.

That's not to say that Georgetta did not travel. Family holidays were taken in Russia or Bulgaria, or of course closer to home in Romania. Fortunately these countries offer a wide variety of climates and landscapes. 'No one felt they were missing anything,' she told me. 'The places we visited were often very nice and I have fond memories of those childhood family holidays.'

Her first job after university was as a technical translator, working for a metallurgical institute. The job entailed working in Spanish, English, French, Romanian and Russian. 'Russian was far from my best language,' she said, 'but my father jokingly told me simply to end every word with a '-ski' and I'd be fine.'

To supplement her salary she also translated books and tutored in the evenings. Home was a small but comfortable apartment in a typically Eastern European block. Passionate about rescuing stray dogs and cats, her home provided sanctuary to an ever-changing population of pets. Her extra work was necessary as she found herself always with many small mouths to feed.

In common with many busy people she had little time for romance. Family, friends and her menagerie of stray animals kept her both occupied and amused. The years rolled by, the Iron Curtain collapsed but for Georgetta, life continued as always, translating, socialising and saving strays.

That changed early in 1998, when, in response to an advertisement in the newspaper, she acquired a pen-friend. Don, an Englishman living in the Midlands had befriended a Romanian couple living near to him and was struck by their stories about life back home. Unmarried, he had at the back of his mind the fact that he might meet a match. Initially though, he simply extended a hand of friendship through that newspaper ad.

The friendship developed and Don visited Bucharest, eventually proposed and then the challenge was to find a way of persuading the authorities to allow Georgetta to move to the UK. Paradoxically whereas for most of her life it was the Romanian authorities that inhibited travel, now it was the UK authorities that made emigration difficult.

Romania was not yet a member of the European Community and so admission to the UK was not a right. She had to apply for a visa and be interviewed at the British embassy in Bucharest. 'The officials were polite but thorough,' she told me, and she had to show them all the letters she had received from Don. 'We had to convince the officials that our relationship was real, and not just fabricated to enable me to live in Britain.' The interviews and questions continued once they had moved to the UK, but at last Georgetta was given British citizenship.

After a spell of living in the Midlands, Georgetta and Don moved to Norfolk. They had originally been attracted here by tourist literature and at first rented a caravan on the coast. They found the area so much to their liking that they eventually bought a house here instead. Don had by this time retired, so Georgetta set out to find a job.

You might imagine that as a skilled translator fluent in five languages finding a job would be easy. Georgetta found that not to be the case. There always seemed to be some reason why she was not short-listed and those she approached for freelance work rarely had the decency to reply. In the end she approached an employment agency in the market town where she lived. They offered her work as a cleaner.

Georgetta is philosoph-ical about her work, feeling that it's better than sitting around doing nothing. 'I also want to earn some money so that I can continue to rescue cats and dogs,' she told me. This lasting passion is amply illustrated by the dog that shares their life. A very agreeable animal, it found Georgetta whilst she was on holiday camping in Spain. When it was time to come home, the dog (which clearly had no owner) had to come too. The necessary documentation and quarantine was expensive, but as Georgetta said, 'I could hardly turn him out of my tent and come home without him.'

A couple of years ago, Georgetta became a British citizen. 'If you decide to live in a foreign country,' she explained, 'you have to embrace its culture and customs and commit yourself to it.' She has little time for the politically correct who encourage immigrants to retain their language and customs. 'If you decide to live in England, you have to become English and speak English. 'When in Rome, do as the Romans do' she concluded.

She was somewhat aghast when, by way of preparing for her citizenship ceremony at County Hall, she was invited to wear her national dress and make use of translators. 'In Romania,' she told me, 'there are 26 ethnic groups each with their own language. Every one of them, however, considers themselves Romanian first and speaks the Romanian language.' She went on to explain that in her view, Britain had lost sight of the reason people came here, of the pioneering spirit with which an Empire was won. 'Britain has done so much for such a small country,' she said, 'yet almost seems embarrassed by its ability to succeed. And why this insistence on multiculturalism anyway? What is wrong with British culture?'

It is ironic that it takes someone who moved here to remind us of our right to celebrate our heritage and history. Georgetta's comments about the country she has chosen as her new home suggest that it's time we accepted who we are as a nation and 'move on' from our past. Times change and historical events, viewed from today's standpoint, can appear very unfair. I wonder what tomorrow's historians will make of 21st century Britain?

So where is home?

Did you know that the UK contains just 1% of the world's population? China on the other hand has 20% and India around 16%. Yet we easily forget that each of those nations is vast and diverse in every sense. You can feel as foreign moving across a large country as you do moving to a new country.

Himu

Born and raised in an area often described as the 'Scotland of the East', Himu's father was a senior civil servant in the British administration. His early schoolteachers were well-endowed matronly English ladies in floral print frocks. He grew up feeling very British. It is only when he tells you that his uncles were all tea growers, a career his family had in mind for him, that you realise that he was born in Assam. Shillong, then its capital, sits amid a landscape not unlike that of the Scottish Highlands. This small town was where his father worked and the young Himu spent his youth.

In common with many bright students, he was educated in a British missionary-run English school and at the age of 16 went to do his arts degree in history and economics in a catholic college in Shillong. Even though he was born to an Indian family his father always encouraged him to learn about British culture and values. He always, therefore, aspired to visit and study in England. As he told me, 'you cannot undo a hundred years of British colonialism in half a generation'.

Himu came to England at the age of 19 and worked as a trainee social worker for a few years until he was seconded to the London School of Economics. There he obtained a Post Graduate Diploma in Applied Social Studies, a course focusing on the management of social care.

He decided not to return to India, but to work here instead. He became a social worker, first in London, then

Northampton and finally in Scotland. Assam had a large Scottish population and he was familiar with the Scottish way. However, he found that the management system didn't suit him, and decided to look instead for a senior position in England.

A management job within Norfolk County Council caught his eye and he applied. He wanted more responsibility and to return to England. 'I also wanted to improve myself,' he told me. 'Promotion was an opportunity to learn and develop as well, of course, as a chance to earn more money and rise to the challenge of a bigger job.'

Norfolk was not somewhere he'd ever visited before. He was warned by one of the interview panel, now Baroness Shepherd, that Norfolk was the 'graveyard of ambition.' This he took as a challenge rather than a threat. He moved to Norwich and has lived there ever since.

That's not to say he abandoned ambition. He worked his way up the career ladder within the Council, becoming one of its most senior managers. By this time he was married with a family and had lived in Britain for more years than he had in India. 'We travelled to India several times,' Himu said, 'to visit family. We also went India as tourists, seeing much of the country for the first time.' India is, after all, a very big place.

Himu's career could easily have plateaued at this point. He had a senior post in the public sector, dealing with some of the most challenging and complex cases that confront a

Social Services department. He felt settled in Norwich and life was good. However, he wanted more from his career and left the security of the public sector at the age of 50 to become a freelance consultant.

Inevitably his first clients were people he already knew, but soon the boundaries widened and he found himself working worldwide. Some might consider it ironic that he has even returned to India to undertake consultancy assignments. To Himu however, Norfolk is his home and India a large country; his birthplace is almost 2,000 miles from Bangalore. (By comparison, Murmansk is 2,000 miles from London!)

However, despite his very traditional British upbringing and more than 30 years living in the UK, Himu is Indian. He was raised bilingual, speaking Bengali and English. 'There are many Indian languages,' he said, 'but everyone speaks English; it is the language of education, commerce and Government.'

Himu has not encountered racism to any great extent. This perhaps is because he has moved in professional circles, less exposed to those with narrow minds and no understanding of the history that inextricably links us with India. It is also fair to say that Norfolk does not have a large Asian community. Perhaps things would be different if it did.

Travelling has given Himu the opportunity to reflect on British life and attitudes. His upbringing in India, study in

England and a career in social services has placed him in a position to see our culture in a unique and objective way. 'We have a strong tendency to fight shy of saying we're fine,' he explained. 'Ask someone how they are and they'll say they're not too bad; never great, happy or successful.'

Our tendency to knock achievement worries Himu. He is more aware than most of the confidence and strength that enabled this small island to build an empire. Today, however, he sees a nation of people reluctant to be positive, reluctant to value achievement and reluctant to recapture its lost pride.

'Life is truly what you make it,' Himu concluded, 'and if you have enthusiasm, drive, pride and principles you can make almost anything happen'. His advice is to focus on what's great about our history, to radiate enthusiasm and to be a positive influence in the world today.

The place we are born and raised is where most of us consider home. How often do you ask someone where they live and hear the reply; 'I live in Norwich but come from XYZ originally.' The Romans even made you go back to your place of birth to be counted when a census took place. If you've read the Christian bible you'll remember that a census plays a major part in the Christmas story.

I was quite late leaving home and setting up my own place. Home, although not desperately happy, was convenient. I lacked the confidence to break away earlier and finally left at the age of 25. My son, on the other hand, went away to University at the age of 18 and has only really been home as a visitor ever since. He prefers his room in a house shared with friends to the greater luxury of the family home.

Others find breaking the link with home a lifelong challenge. This is particularly true of people for whom independent living can be a challenge. People with enduring mental health problems often remain living with parents well into middle age. In time though, almost everyone wants to set up a place of their own that they can call home.

Gerald

A Londoner by birth, Gerald did well at school and studied English and Greek civilisation at University. He was like thousands of other bright graduates, although less driven than many to explore and perhaps change the world.

On graduation he found a job in local government and life fell into a comfortable routine. He still lived with his family. Remaining there seemed easier than branching out on his own. Always close to his mother, he found it difficult to find girlfriends able to meet both his and her expectations.

Gerald is not sure what caused his first spell of depressive illness. He suspects it was a combination of factors, not least the belligerence and pride that meant he could not readily accept things as they are, preferring instead to seek change, albeit on a modest scale.

His boss attributed Gerald's growing depression to the stress of his job and offered to reduce his responsibilities, but not his pay, so that he could work through his problems. Unfortunately anti-depressants did not help and he spent time as a voluntary patient in a psychiatric hospital.

The regime at hospital was very different from psychiatric care today. 'You had to get up,' he told me, 'and eat your meals, whether you were hungry or not'. He went on to explain that the paradox of this daily routine was that there was little to do when you were up, apart from watch TV. Today, it seems, life is more relaxed in hospital and if you feel like spending the day in bed alone, there is no real pressure to do otherwise.

With no real diagnosis of his illness, Gerald struggled on and eventually took the decision to commit suicide. Looking back on it now he is almost embarrassed that he tried to escape his illness in this way. It is only due to an amazing and macabre coincidence that he is alive today.

Having stockpiled his medication he travelled to Cirencester and booked into a very pleasant hotel. When he checked in he ordered a morning paper, not expecting to be alive to read it. 'I thought I would appear more normal if I ordered a paper,' he said. 'I didn't want to draw attention to myself.'

After an evening of heavy drinking, Gerald decided it was time to go. He went to his room, took all the pills he had brought with him, lay down and waited.

He came round in the emergency treatment room at Swindon Hospital. Unbeknown to him, another guest had killed himself at the hotel the day before Gerald arrived. The staff noticed Gerald's newspaper outside the door at 9am and when he didn't answer their knock on the door went in and found him unconscious; a macabre example of once bitten, twice shy.

When he had recovered sufficiently he was moved back to the psychiatric hospital he had voluntarily attended before. Even then he was not diagnosed and it was only later in a private clinic that he was told he was manic depressive. You might say that surely this was obvious. Gerald's response is to point out that symptoms can be common to several illnesses and it is not as easy as diagnosing an ulcer or broken leg.

Then Gerald's father died. There was no pension or life insurance and to make their money go further, Gerald and his mother moved to Norfolk to make a fresh start. Norfolk had been home to some of Gerald's forbearers so he felt an affinity with the place. His illness continued as did occasional spells in hospital. Whilst the regime is gentler these days, he told me that electro-convulsive therapy is still used today: little has really changed.

Gerald has found the arts a help; being busy stops him feeling ill. He plays the piano and sings in a choir. Others he knows paint or write; the mediums often providing what he calls, 'valuable insights into their delusions.' The role of art is well-known in the treatment of mental illness. 'People tend to keep their mad thoughts to themselves,' Gerald confided, 'otherwise people know you're not well.'

Although he will always be manic depressive Gerald prefers the company of people who are not ill. There is what he calls a 'manic depressive's fellowship' of what the medical profession euphemistically call 'service users', who hang around together reinforcing each others' symptoms.

Gerald's mother is now 81 and both have decided he should start to make his own life without her. He recently moved into a flat from a bedsit in a social housing complex where support was on hand should he need it. At the age of 55 it's his first spell of independent living.

He visits his mother most weekends, but now returns to his own place at night. 'She needs space of her own,' he told me, 'and I want to find myself a girlfriend and think about settling down.'

Gerald's story is not uncommon. Nor is it a story told only by people with poor mental health. Italian men are renowned for being late to leave their mothers' cooking and set up home on their own. Home can seem like a good place to be and time can just drift by, almost unnoticed.

When we met Gerald said how important singing and music was to his mental health. He probably knows more about classical music than anyone else I know. He also loves

 singing in a choir. Reflecting on our conversation I was reminded of a very powerful event I witnessed some years ago at Findhorn. There is much said about this long established eco-community in North East Scotland; not all of it positive! That said, I attended a weekend conference there and on Sunday morning found myself alone on a balcony overlooking the foyer to the settlement's community centre.

People began arriving and soon there were around 100 folk, young and old, gathered together. They then began to sing hauntingly beautiful, harmonious, Scandinavian pieces that really reach in and touch your soul. There really is something magical about a crowd of people singing together especially if you are one of that crowd. Belonging to a choir can create that sense of belonging we all crave.

Gerald's choir is associated with the local mental health hospital. He introduced me to Tracy, a psychotherapist who set the choir up some time ago. It's a voluntary group, reliant on grants for funding and meets at the hospital mainly because they don't charge. Choir members come from both the hospital community and from the city. Some have mental health problems, many don't; they just love that sense of belonging that membership of a choir provides.

Tracy

Tracy is one of those people who sees an opportunity and takes it. Always fascinated by people, she first trained as a psychiatric nurse. She is also interested in oral history and the way knowledge and attitudes are passed down from one generation to the next.

As her career developed she trained as a psychotherapist, working with in-patients at the hospital. 'Music can get right into your emotions' she told me, 'and there were few real opportunities for patients here to play music or sing.'

'Sing Your Heart Out' now attracts around 50 people to its singing workshops. They have a professional coach and rehearse and perform works that are easy for the untrained voice. The idea is to enjoy making music together, not become proficient performers of challenging works!

Members of the choir include hospital staff, former and current patients and people who simply want to sing. Singing together breaks down barriers and reduces stigma. As Gerald once told me, 'the only reason now that we meet at the hospital is because some of our singers would find it difficult being let out to sing in the city!'

Belonging, then, is important to us all. As children, most of us feel we are members of a family. In adulthood, we create our own places of safety; places to live as well as places to be with others, sharing experiences and feeling valued. Home to me, quite simply, is anywhere I feel I belong.

Do you feel that you belong? What about your friends and family? Here are three things to talk about with the people you feel close to:

What makes a place a home? Home is much more than a place, it's a feeling too. Discuss your home with others and see how your views of home differ.

Why are people important to you – When you think about Princess Diana you realise that there was someone who was very unhappy, despite having material wealth. What makes you happy and how can you help others feel happy too?

Singing is just one example of an activity that makes people feel they belong – discuss with a group of friends what makes you all feel that you belong. Are there things you could start or develop that might make it easy for new people to join your circle of friends?

Four

Vulnerability

"When we were children, we used to think that when we were grown-up we would no longer be vulnerable. But to grow up is to accept vulnerability... To be alive is to be vulnerable".

Madeleine L'Engle
"Walking on Water: Reflections on Faith and Art", 1980

One of my heroes is the management writer Charles Handy. He is a good bit older than me, which makes it possible to benchmark my career as an author against his. He left industry to research and write about management. Latterly, his focus has moved away from processes to write about people; extraordinary people who do extraordinary things.

His wife Liz is a professional photographer. She was for many years a counsellor with Relate and this gives her an amazing ability to connect with people. She is one of the most encouraging people I know, able to touch lives just by being there.

I commissioned Liz to produce a portrait of my family, in our home, to mark my 50th birthday. She creates what she calls 'joiners' - photo-montages in the style of David Hockney. She captured us doing ordinary day-to-day things, then combined them to form the portrait.

At one point in our email exchanges as we planned the shoot, the subject of mental health came up. I mentioned to her that I lived with depression and had undergone three years of psychotherapy. Her response was to thank me for revealing my vulnerability to her.

As I reflected on the comment, the penny dropped. I realised something I'd overlooked for my entire life. The simple fact is that the more you allow others to see your vulnerability, the more comfortable they will be letting you see theirs.

In other words, the more you hide your vulnerabilities the less human you appear. Uniformity, what happens when we all seem the same, dehumanises us and makes unacceptable behaviour seem OK. It's why soldiers wear uniforms; you're then shooting a soldier and not a man!

I've certainly learned since that day the true value of allowing others to see your vulnerabilities. It makes you a better partner, parent, manager and friend. It enables you to connect with people in new and intimate ways.

Being timid

Some people are largely defined by their vulnerability. It is the most obvious thing about them as you get to hear their story. To say, 'for goodness sake pull your socks up and get out there' is not going to help them. Nor will you win their trust by projecting a secure, bombproof, untouchable façade that they will find both daunting and impenetrable. We can learn a lot from people who appear vulnerable and timid. They often have a sensitivity to the world that makes them acutely aware of their surroundings. Those of us who are bolder and sometimes unfeeling can learn a lot from them.

Stanley

Stanley was born in Norwich in 1929. His parents had started married life in a converted railway carriage, moving to a new council house a couple of years before Stanley was born. They were typical of their generation; honest, hard working, decent folk who managed with what they had. There was little money for luxuries.

When war broke out, Stanley watched wide-eyed as the windows were taped and blackout curtains made. 'I was a sensitive child,' he told me, 'quite shy and I didn't like parties.' The notion of air raids must have seemed terrifying to ten year-old Stanley.

On 2nd August 1942 his father was killed in an air raid. His mother was away at the time; she'd just given birth to

Stanley's youngest sister. The news was broken by his granny. He was just thirteen years old, with two older siblings at work and a four year-old brother. There were no social workers to offer support. He just had to manage as best he could until his mother returned.

At 14 he left school and got a job in a garage. He found he loved stripping and restoring engines. 'I felt very proud when the starter was pressed and it started first time,' he said.

Conscription to the army was another difficult time. 'I found it very hard being shouted at on the barrack square,' he explained. 'Also, being with lots of people made it nearly too much for me to bear,' he added. It really is tough, in today's world, to imagine what it must have been like to be forced to spend two years in the armed forces; to have no choice.

Sometimes, when he went home for the weekend, Stanley would try to scald himself. Self harming was in those days a way of avoiding having to return to camp. The reluctant soldier would also miss meals as he couldn't face going to the cookhouse where there were so many people. One day, under threat of a visit to the guard-house if he continued to refuse, Stanley fought another man in the boxing ring. He suffered a broken tooth; a lasting reminder of a very unpleasant experience.

Demobbed at 20, Stanley returned to his job as a mechanic in Norwich and threw himself into his work. He was hugely relieved to be away from the bustle of the army. He was now even more determined to avoid crowds.

Success at work created more challenges. He was invited to go to the Standard Motor Company in Coventry for a fort-night. As a star mechanic his boss wanted him train with the car makers' team. 'I panicked and decided I could not go,' he told me. 'I was seeing a psychiatrist by then and he advised me to admit myself to hospital.'

In 1961 the mental hospital was a daunting Victorian building with long wide corridors. As Stanley walked up the drive, he saw patients working in the fields around the building. He was terrified of being attacked.

Although a voluntary patient, Stanley was shocked to find himself in hospital. He described how he withdrew from reality and wanted to die. Treatment here and at another hospital seemed to focus on sedation and group therapy. There was also occupational therapy.

After nearly two years Stanley decided he wanted to leave and get a job. He was advised against this but as a voluntary patient was able to discharge himself. He held down a low-paid job for a couple of months before being re-admitted to hospital.

Stanley wondered if ECT would help and asked the question. He was given two doses but neither helped. It seems amazing today that such severe treatments could be administered in such a seemingly cavalier way. Eventually, though, Stanley did get better, left hospital and returned to work.

He met his wife when running a social club for nervous people in Norwich. They married in secret, although both families approved. Finally, Stanley got an administrative job at City Hall and stayed there for nineteen years. He was made redundant shortly before retirement and now, at last, as a pensioner has the opportunity to live life as he wants.

Critics might say that Stanley has achieved little with his life. Others might say that he is a product of his upbringing and stood little chance. What all would agree is that for whatever reason, Stanley has always felt vulnerable.

His life was constantly being taken over by forces beyond his control. Childhood nights in a cold Anderson Shelter, waiting for the bombs to fall; conscription and the unthinking hell of enforced captivity with crowds he'd rather avoid, then finally, when he admitted defeat, a treatment regime that seems rudimentary by today's standards.

If Stanley had been born 30 years later he would have avoided the war, avoided conscription, experienced better care and would certainly have faced more opportunity. More significantly perhaps, he would have been respected for his vulnerabilities and not forced to conform.

Of course Norfolk is full of people who have faced similar life challenges. Most have fortunately been better able to cope. That's not to say it's Stanley's fault that he has found life difficult, nor is it his 'fault'. In my view he was simply born less well prepared than the majority to deal with the societal events that so affected his life.

Shit happens

None of us can predict when we're going to face personal challenge. Life can seem to be totally under control, with everything organised and a great future lined up, when shit happens. Forgive the bluntness, but life can be shit at times and there's no point in saying otherwise.

Some spend a lifetime preparing for tomorrow, only to be robbed of a future by death or disabling sickness. My own parents fell into this trap. Even in their 40s, they were planning their retirement. The places they would visit; the things they would do. Both became ill and both died in their early 50s. Their dream became their children's inheritance. We'd have preferred them to be happy.

It is too easy as you walk through an affluent, buzzing city centre like Norwich to assume that everyone you pass has lived a life like yours. In reality, nothing could be further from the truth. Stop some passers by and ask them to share their life story and you'll be amazed by the diversity of experience.

Genocide

For centuries Norwich has been a place of refuge. Flemish Huguenots came there in the 17th century to escape religions persecution, setting the scene for later, smaller influxes of asylum seekers. The university attracts students from across the world and that itself brings others here too.

Norwich is home to a number of survivors of the holocaust. An event in recent history so horrible that even for those of us born years later, mankind's collective memory of it still reverberates through us all.

However, it is more recent examples of genocide that hit us harder. The holocaust took place when my parents were children; the Rwandan genocide took place when I was an adult. Sure it was a long way away, but could I, and those around me, have done anything to lessen the impact of this and other events? I guess potentially yes.

Illuminée

Illuminée lives in Norwich. She was born into a modestly affluent Catholic family who lived in a suburb of the Rwandan capital. She grew up in a happy community with neighbour helping neighbour.

But at the age of 11 she realised that she was different. Her teacher asked all students to raise their hands if they were Tutsis. Illuminée along with a few others put their hands up. The majority of the class were Hutus.

Her Tutsi 'badge' meant that she failed the entrance exam for secondary school. As she told me, only Hutus passed the exam, virtually all Tutsis failed. That act of racist discrimination was the first inkling she had that she was a second class citizen in Rwanda.

The wedge that divided Hutu and Tutsi was driven by European colonialism. Before then the two groups, who shared the same language and culture, had lived harmoniously. Since before Illuminée was born, however, periodic outbreaks of racial tension and violence had damaged her country, an otherwise prosperous nation by African standards.

Her parents paid for private education and she stayed at school, living at home until she met her husband, John. He was the widower of a close friend who had died in childbirth. It was a tragic event, but not as tragic as what was to follow later.

Early 1994 found Illuminée living with her husband, pregnant with their child, planning their wedding, which took place on 3 April. Then the genocide started following the death of President Habyarimana in a plane crash on 6 April.

Illuminée gave birth to their son, Roger, at John's aunt's house on 1 May. But they could not stay there and returned home. John bravely went out to try and find some pain-killers. Then the Interahamwe (Hutu militia) stormed the house looking for her husband. He was not there so they left empty handed. Unlike many Tutsi women she was not raped, a fact she attributes to having just given birth. But the Interahamwe gang raped the young woman who helped in their house. Outside the troubles escalated and bodies were piled on the streets, butchered with machetes.

Then the Interahamwe called once more. This time John was at home. He knew all his adversaries – friends and neighbours in happier days. John was taken away and killed. Illuminée was told later that a friend who had been at their wedding chopped off John's arms before he was shot.

Illuminée's next move was perhaps even more chilling. The Interahamwe took her to John's aunt's home. The local Interahamwe leader had looked after their children while the adults were killed. Illuminée was ordered to take over. Even today, she asks herself what kind of logic directed the Interahamwe leader to be so concerned about the children his men had just orphaned.

During the remaining months of the genocide, Illuminée had many close encounters with death. One day, she was taken to a roadblock manned by an execution squad. However, perhaps sickened by all the killing, they could not be bothered to do their work.

In a bizarre twist an Interahamwe leader protected her and eventually she started the journey to Zaire, along with thousands of terrified Tutsi refugees. However she was rescued by the victorious Tutsi-led Rwandan Patriotic Front and returned to Kigali. Had she made it to Zaire, (DR Congo) she believes she would have died. Tens of thousands perished in the squalid, disease-ridden plains of Goma, where those who'd fled gathered.

Illuminée lost her husband, one sister and many other friends and relatives in the genocide. Life could never be the same again. She had a baby to raise and was determined to give him every chance of a better life. His father may have died, but her son was going to live a life free of violence and despair.

Illuminée's cousin, Esther, had worked for Oxfam before the genocide. When peace returned the aid agencies came back. Esther resumed her job and in 1996 was offered the opportunity to come to the University of East Anglia to study. Illuminée accompanied Esther, working as her nanny, looking after Esther's three children and Roger. This was Illuminée's first trip out of Rwanda. She was bilingual, speaking French, and had worked for a time as an interpreter. However she did not speak English and was ill-prepared for the climate and culture she encountered in Norfolk.

When Esther returned to Rwanda, Illuminée stayed. Her son was getting on well and she felt he faced a better future in Norfolk than Rwanda. They both applied for full British citizenship, which was finally granted in 2002.

However the stresses of living in a strange country had a serious effect on her mental health. Illuminée was diagnosed as suffering from post-traumatic stress disorder.

It took several years for the effect of the genocide to diminish. Illuminée says she will never fully recover; the experience was simply too horrific for that. Her son on, the other hand, has become a typical British schoolboy. Now 14, he is aware of his heritage, but equally aware that Britain is his home. He is fully integrated and to hear him speak, you would assume he'd been born here. In some ways perhaps, he was.

Illuminée has ambitions. She is studying catering and wants to open a Rwandan-style restaurant in Norwich. She's done her research and is sure there's a market. First, though, she has to escape. Not from genocide this time, but from what is termed the 'benefit trap'. Throughout her illness and recovery, she has lived in a council flat, supported by various benefits. This, together with the stigma of having suffered a spell of mental ill-health, makes it difficult to climb out of where she is and start her own business. She remains stoical though; she has survived far worse.

The irony of Illuminée's situation illustrates graphically how prejudice and stigma, even in Norwich, can hold someone back from realising a dream. Here is a woman who has survived genocide, learned English and overcome so many obstacles. Yet despite all that, getting the support she needs to become financially independent is proving to be the most difficult challenge of all to counter. It seems that Norwich, as well as Illuminée, needs that Rwandan restaurant!

Getting help

There's nothing worse than that feeling of helplessness. Feeling vulnerable, misunderstood, bullied or just very sensitive is not nice. It can affect not only your mental health, but your physical health can also suffer. Stress can be bad for your heart. Comfort eating can also pile on the pounds, and the misery.

For most of us, the hardest step to take is to accept we have a problem; or perhaps not so much a problem as a desire to see our challenges in a new light. That way we can learn to be less affected by those around us and more confident in being ourselves.

The doctor's surgery is a good place to start although getting your problem across in one ten minute appointment can be a challenge! The NHS has a wide range of services at its disposal to help you over life's emotional hurdles. They are certainly better today than they were in Stanley's day. Illuminée's story, however, suggests that more could be done.

As you might expect, there are many private counsellors and therapists of all kinds. These are people who have made it their business to help others. Just like doctors, some are better than others. If you can afford it and seek help of this kind, it's vital to meet several possible providers before making your choice.

Sue

With an array of qualifications and a wealth of experience, Sue spends her working life helping people. Her website says that she specialises in helping people find solutions to stress, depression, eating disorders, relationship problems and post-traumatic stress. She has a thriving private practice, with many clients referred to her by local doctors and psychologists.

Like so many of us, Sue's career was shaped by her child-hood experience. 'When I was born, my brother was not expecting a sister,' she explained, 'so he made my life a misery.' Although the abuse never went beyond bullying, Sue's childhood was shaped by her brother's actions. 'I had to learn to transform his negative energy into something positive,' she told me. Today, she has no contact with her brother at all; they've agreed on that at least.

Sue now lives and works in Norfolk. She came here because her parents lived here. By now a single parent with a son, she wanted him to benefit from being part of a family. She also wanted her parents to have the chance to help rear her son, giving her some opportunity to develop her career.

Apart from dealing with people coming to terms with their mistreatment by others, she also finds people damaged by kindness. Well, the actions that others deemed to be kind. 'How dare we assume,' she exclaimed angrily, 'to know what's right for someone else!'

She tells the story of a lady she knows who rescued her learning-disabled twin sister from care. It's rather like that Dustin Hoffman film 'Rain Man', where Hoffman plays an autistic man living in a care home who inherits his father's fortune. His brother, who did not know he even existed, befriends him to gain access to his money. Sue's client's motive was more altruistic, but no less compelling. Times change and we no longer hide away those who do not match our perception of perfection!

Sue is fascinated by happiness and the individuality that makes one person's happiness another person's hell. 'You simply can't impose your expectations on others,' she declared, 'because when it comes to being happy, there is not really any right or wrong answer.'

In common with so many in the caring professions, Sue is driven by a strong sense of justice. She wants to see people having more choice over the way they lead their lives. She would be appalled by Stanley's experiences, knowing the lasting damage that forcing someone to undergo any regime can cause. The tragedy is that there are simply not enough people like Sue to go round. Even those able to pay can find it hard to find someone able to help them. We need more people like Sue and moreover, a more tolerant world where people can be themselves, free of the oppressive influence of others.

What makes you feel vulnerable? Or how about the people you care most about? Here are three things to explore:

What makes you feel vulnerable – it could be at home, work or within your local community. How does your response to these things amplify or diminish the feelings?

Who do you know who lived through the Second World War? – How did the experience shape them? What are the differences between your views and theirs? Why do you think this is?

How can you spot when those around you are vulnerable and may need help? Discuss with friends what symptoms and signs might show that someone feels vulnerable? How can you help them without interfering or using your own values to influence them?

Five

Recovery

'A slip of the foot you may soon recover, but a slip of the tongue you may never get over.'

Benjamin Franklin 1706 - 1790

When people talk about recovery they can mean different things. Usually, they are referring to some illness or disadvantage that has befallen you. But sometimes that disadvantage is more in their perception than your reality.

When our friends catch a cold we say, 'get well soon,' and that's fine. When something more significant takes place, the death of a partner for example, wishing a speedy recovery is harder. In that scenario, their life will improve as they come to terms with the loss. It will never though 'recover' to where it was before.

Worse for me is when people assume that because you are different in some way, you must want to recover to be just like everybody else.

Periodically I suffer from bouts of depression. These are never very severe and rarely stop me working for more than a day or two. Yet people ask me when I will recover from this illness that in their view must blight my life.

My view of this condition is somewhat different. My "down" weeks are times of remarkable insight and introspection. They enable me to understand myself and to review where and who I am. My "up" weeks burst with creativity, intuition and courage. These are the times when I have my best ideas and more importantly, sell them to others.

Would I really trade this life full of wonderful contrast for something altogether more bland? Do I really want to be just like everyone else? How can anyone else actually know what it's like living inside my head and riding my own very personal, virtual rollercoaster? No, they have no idea and why should they? To change in such a profound way is a form of recovery no-one can wish on another human being, however good an idea it seems.

People with more severe mental health problems may well hope for more control over their emotions and behaviours. Having voices in your head, making huge demands of you, can be very, very wearing. But even these people in my experience rarely complain about being ill. They simply want us to recognise that life for them is different.

Society is in many ways to blame for our attitudes to recovery. From an early age we are encouraged to conform. What we are encouraged to conform to is, of course, a variable. Political regimes, cultural traditions and environmental factors change. Today's acceptable behaviour was yesterday's imprisonable offence. Ask any gay man aged over 70 if you don't believe me! He will have risked prosecution as a young man to do what today is socially acceptable and legal in every respect.

Society's intolerance

Rules are vital if any semblance of order is to be maintained. Yet the way those rules are interpreted is vital if we are to recognise that illness and disability can change the need for those rules to be enforced. When someone really is ill and recovery impossible, a compassionate and caring society would flex the rules to recognise changing circumstances.

Mary

Mary is 76 and has lived in Norwich all her life. Her father worked for the football club and she has fond childhood memories of watching the team play after they moved to Carrow Road.

Her parents taught her from an early age to, 'never start a task until you know you can do it properly.' This discouragement from experimentation made Mary something of a perfectionist. Trial and error was not acceptable to her. Her aversion to risk was probably exacerbated by the fact that her father had been shot in the First World War. He had volunteered as a teenager and been shot and wounded after a couple of years at the front.

Mary contacted me because she wanted to share her experiences of severe depression with me. Widowed in her 60s she had thrown herself into voluntary work and was active in a number of roles around the city. As for her mental health, it would be almost too easy to attribute her depression to a lifetime quest for perfection. She admitted to always having set very high standards for herself and often, this battle against second best can tip you into depression.

Over a cup of coffee she gave me chapter and verse about her condition. She has experienced a wide spectrum of services designed to help her recover; drugs, therapies and doctors of all kinds. It seems unnecessary to relay those experiences to you; they are very much Mary's business and not for us to pick over.

What was far more relevant to the theme of this book was one of her volunteering roles; Mary is a prison visitor. Furthermore she is not just any prison visitor, but someone who befriends some of the men held in the specialist geri-

atric unit at Norwich prison. This is essentially a nursing home behind bars for prisoners too infirm for mainstream jail, but with more time to serve behind bars before they can be released.

Perhaps the most notorious of these prisoners is Ronnie Biggs. He was jailed in the 1960s for his part in the Great Train Robbery, the audacious hold up of a mail train where a record sum of money (£2.3m) was stolen. His notoriety was enhanced when he escaped from prison after just 15 months and fled to Brazil, where he stayed for 30 years.

According to media interviews with his son Michael, Biggs is now 78 years old, partially paralysed and virtually unable to speak having suffered a couple of strokes. 'He clearly represents no danger to society whatsoever', his son told reporters as he campaigns to have him released. Whether or not you feel Biggs should be allowed out to die with his family is not the issue. It is the fact that our society's rules make it an issue is my concern.

Rightly, Mary could not tell me much about her work at the prison, except to say that she did it. She visits many lonely old men who live in that closed care environment. Some I guess have no family on the outside and if released would simply exchange one state funded institution for another. She did, however, mention that the unit also housed a couple of younger men, severely disabled by failed suicide attempts in prisons. That to me seems the biggest tragedy of all.

Mary closed by telling me that when these men are released, she never hears from or of them again. It's as if they take her friendship and support, yet when released never write to say thank you. Perhaps it should be suggested when they are finally released. Although prisoners never know the visitor's address, they could write to them care of the prison.

People who have broken the rules and been punished, yet become physically ill to the point that they no longer appear to represent a risk pose an interesting conundrum. Recovery for them in a physical sense is not possible. Recovery of dignity and an opportunity where possible to see out their days with family is achievable, but is it acceptable?

Secrets

The recovery of childhood innocence is something many of us would wish for ourselves. However once that innocence has been lost, it can never be recovered, however much we wish for it.

Child abuse, in all its forms, robs children of their sexual innocence even if they are too young to fully understand. It damages the lives of both victim and perpetrator, often making recovery impossible, even with lots of professional support.

However childhood innocence can be surrendered in far more ways than this. Secrets kept from a child then innocently discovered can change a life for ever. The moment of revelation becomes firmly embossed on the memory never to be erased.

Denise

Denise had an idyllic childhood. A neat and tidy bungalow home, new car, a cruiser on the Broads and a caravan; it was very much a 'Swallows and Amazons' experience. Home was comfortable, her parents were kind and loving and everything was perfect.

There was only one place Denise was forbidden to go. That was a drawer in the sideboard where 'private things' were kept by her parents. 'For as long as I can remember, Mum and Dad used to say, don't go in there,' she told me.

However, children are naturally inquisitive and in time, her curiosity got the better of her. She was actually 15 when she finally decided to take a look and see what it was that she was not supposed to see.

'Mum and Dad had gone out,' she explained, 'and I knelt down and opened the drawer really slowly, just in case they'd done something that would show I'd taken a look inside,' she added.

There was no trap or trick and opening the drawer fully she saw it was simply full of brown official looking envelopes. Most looked uninteresting and Denise began to wonder what it was she was not supposed to be seeing. Then she saw it; an envelope bearing the words 'private papers', melodramatically written on the front.

Inside she found old photographs of a young boy. An only child, she had no idea who this was so looked further. Then she spotted a yellowing newspaper cutting. It reported the death by drowning of a ten year old boy. This event took place when she was three years old. Later, she discovered that this boy was her step-brother. He had never been mentioned.

Further rummaging revealed her birth certificate. She unfolded it hesitantly and saw a blank where her father's name should have been written. 'Why had they never told me about the little boy? If my father is not my father, then who is? I had so many questions,' she exclaimed.

Denise carefully re-packed the drawer with its now-revealed secrets. She had crossed a line that could never be re-crossed, knowledge from which there could never be a recovery.

Months later she could live with her feelings of guilt no longer. She put her arms around her father and confessed. 'I felt so ashamed,' she told me, 'and heartbroken that this man I loved as a father was not in fact my dad.' Denise went on to describe how her father hugged her tight and said that no matter what, she would always be his little girl. Tears were shed.

Her parents later explained that the dead child had been her father's son from his first marriage. He had married her mother after she had been born. Although not her natural father Denise pushed the sad fact that he was not to the back of her mind. Why search for the real one, she mused, when this man is my dad in every other way.

Life recovered in many ways until three years later he hanged himself. Her mother had a new man who quickly entered her life. Angry, ashamed and confused, Denise walked out. She did not see her mother again for nine long years.

Today, Denise is happily married with two wonderful children. She works hard to give her two youngsters the carefree happy childhood she had until opening the drawer changed it for ever.

'Our house may not be perfect,' she told me, 'but it is our home. I try to instil in my children the values my Mum and Dad taught me. I want them to treasure them as I did'.

Time healed the worst of the trauma for Denise and she now enjoys a reasonably good relationship with her mother. They go shopping together and do those other harmless things that grown-up daughters do with their mothers. Both have been scarred by the past and neither really wants to remember. For them, recovery is about breaking the chain, so that her children never experience the same pain that she felt.

Families

Both as a child and now as a parent, Denise has focused herself on her family. Our family is, after all, the place where we are entitled to expect unconditional acceptance, love and support. It's a tough package to deliver as any parent knows. It is also a lifelong commitment, ending perhaps when the parents reach that stage of life where the tables are turned and come to rely more and more on their offspring for guidance and support.

Siblings are something different. I have both a brother and a sister and am estranged from them both. I bullied my brother and my sister, being nine years younger, grew up not really knowing me at all. I've not spoken to her for more than 20 years and no longer even have her address.

Until I started sharing this fact with others, I thought that sibling separation of this kind was unusual and in some way my fault. I now realise that it's not at all unusual and the result of a combination of factors, not least the fact that our father was an alcoholic bank manager. Between nine and five he was a pillar of the local community. At night, he was a very different animal.

As I grow older I increasingly regret the missed opportunities to share life's episodes with my siblings. We are all married, all have children and have all done well in our careers. Since our parents died more than 25 years ago, we have all missed out on the perceived benefits of family support and encouragement.

David

The 42 year old manager of a mental health project, David has a very healthy sense of humour. He probably needs it as every working day throws out fresh, unforeseen challenges. But then his whole life has been punctuated by people challenges, starting with his family.

He describes his family as 'normal and dysfunctional.' It makes you wonder if normal can only be found in works of fiction. His brother bullied him when they were boys, perhaps more severely than most. David describes the relationship as violent and chooses not to expand on the matter.

In early adulthood, David's brother abused himself with drugs and alcohol. He became psychotic and spent many months in various mental health institutions. He died ten years ago. David was initially more fortunate, suffering from panic attacks and depression. 'My panic attacks could last for days,' he confided, 'and I started drinking to ease the anxiety.'

His early career was in local Government. It was a work environment where he found it easy to conceal both his anxiety and his drink habit. Having witnessed his brother's decline he recognised the need to get help. He invested hard-earned savings in private psychiatric consultations. He also underwent group therapy.

David's problems worsened and he was admitted to hospital. He was treated, and at times not treated, in several mental health units. At one stage he was in the same ward as his brother. He described that as 'a surreal experience'. I guess for their parents it was even harder to handle.

He managed to keep his job, commuting to and from hospital to work. Few manage to combine their job with residential psychiatric treatment, but David was determined. Later, as he began to recover, he moved into sheltered accommodation. 'I was 20,' he told me, 'and living with two nutters pushing 60. We had little in common,' he exclaimed.

He first experienced real stigma years later, when he had returned to full health. His experiences of mental health care had been mixed and this had prompted him to find work in the sector. 'For some reason dealing with a former service user as a fellow professional was really difficult for some people,' he told me. 'They simply refused to respect me as an equal.'

Others have told me similar stories. It seems that the medical profession can be very hierarchical and the patient occupies the lowest point in the pecking order as many see it. David does not entirely blame the medics for this. He described for me the phenomenon of the "professional" service user – people with a chip on their shoulder who readily volunteer to represent their class on various mental health consultative groups.

David now manages a service he used when he was ill. His personal experience of life on the 'other side of the fence' equips him well to cope with the realities of his role. Some of that service's clients were there when he was also a client. They are generally accepting of his recovery and choice of career. The suspicion mostly lies on the professionals' side of the fence.

Regret

We all make decisions we live to regret. Hindsight is regrettably not something we are born with. Each and every one of us has to make potentially life-changing decisions without knowing if time will reveal that decision to have been good or bad.

Intuition, our inner voice, can often guide us effectively as we make choices in life. For me, there is often a conflict between the factual evidence I can see and the intuitive feelings I have about a decision I need to make.

When we find we've make a bad decision, we want to wind the clock back. However it is usually impossible to recover what could have been. Time can heal a damaged relationship, but changing jobs and then wishing you hadn't, is tough; here, you usually have to make the best of where you are.

In the weeks where I am feeling particularly low, I can spend hours pondering over decisions already made. Having booked a holiday in France recently I decided to miss the ten hour drive and fly from Stansted to La Rochelle instead. For weeks afterwards, I reflected on the choice I had made. I hate airports, yet the flight takes just 50 minutes.

In reality I can change my mind and drive, forgoing the already paid-for flights. I know, though, that every mile of the way I'd be thinking about the plane I could have been on, visualising my paid-for empty seat. Wishing I was there. I know that if I fret long enough the dilemma will spoil the holiday. I guess we all get these thoughts stuck in our heads.

Stephen

Stephen left Norwich to take a better job in Ipswich. He could have stayed and waited for the right opportunity in Norfolk but was tempted by the opportunity when he saw it advertised. Norwich born and bred, he loves the city yet moving to grow his career seemed the right thing to do. In many ways he did what he thought was right.

The new job meant more money, more responsibility and an opportunity for a fresh start. It was a totally new organisation to him, although very similar to the one he was leaving. It also meant moving his family to Ipswich. That was the decision he came to regret.

Steve's move to Ipswich took place in 1989 and even today, he wants to move back to Norwich. He's never lost his affection for the city, nor has his family. The rivalry between the two communities runs deep although, to be fair, it is small beer when compared with somewhere like Belfast! That said, Norwich represents the heart of Norfolk (or the North Folk) and Ipswich the heart of Suffolk (the South Folk). You only have to see the tension and raw emotion when their respective football teams meet to know that this is tribalism at its finest!

In practical everyday terms, this means that living in either community, exposes you to frequent reminders of the other. It's not overt, more that the subject often comes up in casual conversation. Like a dripping tap, you can be worn down by it if you feel you are living on the wrong side of the River Waveney.

Homesickness, however, is not what wore Stephen down. It was the job. Or to be more precise the couple of promotions and a secondment that led to a position with significant responsibility. He was ably qualified for the job and loved the challenge. What he found trying was that despite an ever-increasing workload, with as he put it, 'everyone

wanting a piece of me.' "Politics" were preventing him from recruiting the right support team. The pressure put him under increasing stress.

'I knew the job would ask a lot of me as there was so much to achieve and so little support,' he explained. 'The job was extremely demanding and a bottomless pit in the amount of work to be done'. The stress mounted and he went off sick.

'I was very tense and felt as if my body was being pulled apart,' he explained, describing how physical the symptoms of his depression became. He took a couple of months off sick, was prescribed anti-depressants and, in his words, 'withdrew'. Things did not improve and apart from novels, nothing interested him. He sought early retirement and this was recently granted.

Free of the stress of work and with his pension sufficient to cover his basic needs, Stephen is planning to move back to Norwich. Once the family has settled in the city, he will look for a job. This time his priority is different; he wants to work to live and not live to work.

Recovery for Stephen was made possible by a number of factors, not least the fact that he was able to take early retirement from a job he enjoyed, but found too much. It is no admission of failure to acknowledge that you can't cope. More the recognition that true success is about being where you want to be, doing things you enjoy, without feeling overwhelmed.

Would you like to turn the clock back and recover lost ground? Or perhaps you need to let go of some remnants of a past life and move on. Why not discuss these questions with someone you trust? See what the conversation provokes.

Are you trapped in a situation (perhaps a relationship, job, or town) that's no longer right for you? Think about what elements are no longer right and how you might change them. Do this with a friend and see if you agree!

How do you feel about your parents? Did they do their best for you? Have you ever thanked them? Are there ways you could improve your relationship with them? Why not give some of them a try?

Have you made decisions you later came to regret? Did they hurt others as well as yourself? What did you learn from them and how can you become better at decision making?

Six

Adapting

'Adapt or perish, now as ever, is nature's inexorable imperative.'

H.G.Wells 1866-1946

We all adapt to changing times without really noticing it. It is only when we are reminded many years later of how things used to be that we realise we have adapted without realising it.

A good example is the classic car. This is particularly true if you are a man aged 50 or over. You may well have fond memories of a car you drove 30 years ago. Perhaps it was your first car. Mine was an Austin 1100. You might remember it as being particularly fast, nimble in traffic, and a very economical run.

Get into the same model car today and you will probably be unpleasantly surprised. For one thing it will seem really small, for another the steering and brakes will not be anywhere near as responsive as you remember. Finally you will be horrified to discover indifferent performance. A small engine that lacks any of today's automotive sophistication is not at all economical to run. 30 miles to the gallon was good in 1963 when petrol was cheap and it didn't really matter.

The thing is that when you traded in your first car it was not for a 21st century replacement. Each car that you bought was slightly better than the one it replaced. As the years rolled by you remembered the good points about the earlier cars and unconsciously forgot the less appealing features.

Life is like that too. As the decades roll by so do our perceptions, expectations and beliefs change also. Almost without noticing, prejudices can grow in our minds to the extent that they eventually influence our behaviour. Social ills such as overcrowding in poor quality accommodation can reduce our tolerance for those we share our space with. Try queuing at an airport on a hot summer's afternoon to see what I mean. People to whom you were polite when you arrived become bitter enemies as the struggle to reach the check-in desk before it closes heats up.

Adapting quickly

Sometimes we dramatically change our attitudes and behaviours as we seek to comply with someone else's rules. Love can be a major driver in this respect. My son only developed a passion for independent cinema when going out with a girl who liked being taken to see alternative films. He soon discovered that her mother shared this interest and was far happier about his relationship with her daughter when he could converse knowledgeably about cinema with her as well.

Religion is another powerful motivator to adapt what we believe and adopt a value set we had previously been happy to ignore. This is compounded if we are making that change because the person we love and want to live with treasures it more than we do.

John

The son of two teachers, John was encouraged by his parents to learn. He sailed through his 11+ and won a free place at the local direct grant Grammar School. However, his father had strong Labour principles and instead, sent John to the local Grammar School instead. As it turned out, this decision was not a problem because John spent much time seriously ill and away from school.

At the age of fourteen he built a telescope. Only the lenses were purchased, the rest being constructed from various materials he was able to acquire. Although he found the world fascinating the universe beyond it also captured his imagination.

Languages also interested him. His mother taught German so it was perhaps inevitable he would learn this too.

She had visited Hamburg shortly after the war and her description of the devastation of that city, and that of the Midlands cities near where he was raised, established his lifelong hatred of war.

After 'A' levels he went on to read Physics. He followed this with a PhD at Warwick where his thesis revolved around the function and improvement of photocopier drums. It was the beginning of a life that would in time lead him further into applied science.

He moved to the US to conduct post-doctoral research in Physics. For a boy who had at times been something of a dissident at school as a man he found the academic environment very comfortable. It was also at this time that he met his wife, then also a post-doctoral researcher. They had much in common although she was American and he British.

At this stage in his life, John took a greater interest in Judaism, largely prompted by his wife's more traditional Jewish upbringing. His parents had brought him up with very secular beliefs but in his mid thirties he felt what he described as a greater affinity with the tribalism of Judaism. He points out that this tiny community is effectively a global nation. 'It is not,' he asserted, 'a faith!' His parents were concerned when his reading around the subject led him to become involved in Jewish affairs, although he points out that he is liberal and pragmatic in his interpretation of Jewish teaching.

He wears both beard and skullcap and so stands out from the crowd. He has, however, never found this a problem and is sufficiently comfortable with his commitment to Judaism to embrace it publicly.

From here the couple moved to a major materials group, where John's research enabled huge savings to be made in the construction of railway carriages. Although the industries were very different, the processes remained largely the same. He had to understand how materials behaved and why. He began writing mathematical algorithms to model quickly what would take a long time to create in an experiment.

The transition from pure to applied physics was not easy. John says that in the 1980s scientists in a large corporate lab could 'pretty much do as they pleased.' He also says that jobs were secure and, for many, corporate life was like being at a university. Companies were prepared to take a long term view and invest in far-reaching research. As the century drew towards its close this attitude changed.

Despite high achievement redundancy became the main precursor for seeking a new challenge. Companies were increasingly downsizing their research teams, or even out-sourcing it completely.

It was the last of these corporate research jobs that brought him to Norfolk. He'd only occasionally visited before and would not have considered it as a place to live. In fact he seriously considered living in Cambridge and commuting. What finally persuaded him was house prices. You could buy more for your money in Norfolk!

The job went well and the family settled down. John's parents, now retired, decided to move up to be near him. Then redundancy struck again. 'I was now living in Norfolk with my parents up the road and no job.' He told me. To find another research job would mean moving again. He and his wife decided to become self-employed.

Working for themselves meant developing new skills. They decided to focus on mathematical modelling, in part because this didn't require a laboratory. He also calculated that if businesses were cutting back on research, his ability to short-cut product development by 'trial and error' through computer simulation would prove popular.

Suspicion, cynicism and inertia became his biggest competitors. He is creatively gifted and so what to him seems obvious can appear daunting and even suspicious to his clients. As is often the case former colleagues became the bedrock of his client base. He had started a part-time MBA before redundancy struck and continued it as he established his own business. Networking and robust market research enabled his business to grow and the couple are close to taking on their second employee.

Confident and in control of his career (no one can now make him redundant) he has started getting involved in local affairs. He recently returned to his boyhood passion of astronomy and bought a powerful telescope. He also established an astronomy club in the town where he lives.

John moved to Norfolk almost by chance, yet has chosen to make it his home. As a Jew he is one of a tiny minority here but that doesn't bother him at all. He knows that, over the centuries, Jews have been persecuted here as they have throughout the world but he carries no chip on his shoulder. John has always felt different from everyone else but has learned to be tolerant of and show interest in what matters to those around him.

History might repeat itself

In many ways our adapting and changing does not really enable mankind to make progress. In my view there is no such thing. What happens is that we move in a large circle returning eventually to where we started but perhaps within a slightly different context.

If you read historical non-fiction you will soon appreciate that people have always been people. We might argue about different things, but the root causes of our argument will be the same basic emotions. Road rage is perhaps an extreme example. Those same feelings that would once have given us the urge, desire and strength to fight someone who is threatening us today fuel our fury against the person who just cut us up on the road. The context today is different but the feelings are just the same.

The decline of the traditional British seaside holiday is, in a way, another example of that cyclical change. Cheap air travel, coupled with our unreliable summer weather, led to people abandoning resorts like Great Yarmouth and Hunstanton to visit Spain and Portugal instead.

Today's rapidly increasing fuel prices, together with a growing fear of skin cancer (or even just sun-induced premature ageing of the skin) is reversing that decades old trend. It is becoming fashionable once more to spend your summer holiday at the British seaside.

David

David was born a few years before the Second World War. His Norfolk village was close to one of the many RAF fighter bases established here when war was expected. He has childhood memories of watching the Spitfires fly out and return. Once, he told me, he saw a plane return on fire; he thinks it landed safely.

His father was an invalid and in the absence of 'the welfare state' his mother's wages from her job as caretaker at the village school was the family's only income. The local church played an important role in their lives. He remembers that on some Sundays the family went to church twice and chapel once!

Despite having little in the material sense, he describes his childhood as a happy one. 'We didn't have much, but neither did we want for much.' He said. Wartime Britain was not a place where much was really possible.

At 14 David moved up from the village school to the larger one in a nearby market town. After a year there he, as did almost everyone at that time, left to find a job. His first job was as a clerk in the town's flour mill. He enjoyed his time there, cycling to and from his village each day. He has no regrets about not having had the chance of further education. He accepts even today that his ability then to add to the family income was more important.

National Service took him out of Norfolk for the first time. The army was very different from life at the mill. However his mother was finding it increasingly difficult to cope with his father's deteriorating health so he was given a compassionate discharge and returned home to help her. 'There was no social care in those days,' he said, 'you had to look after your own.'

He didn't go back to the mill, though, commuting instead to a job in Norwich. Here he also met his wife, a girl born and bred on the coast. When romance led to marriage they decided to set up home in her home town. His parents moved there too to be near them. His father needed him now more than before. They also thought the sea air would help his father's failing health.

During their early years in their new home, the traditional seaside holiday was still in full swing. Entire Midlands factories would close down for a fortnight allowing workers to holiday together at the coast. In those days, the town had three railways stations and five theatres. Each theatre was packed throughout the season. The town was enjoying its heyday.

David took a job with a local firm that supplied catering equipment. His work took him to the many hotels and guest-houses around the town. 'All did well,' he told me. 'The place was busy for all of the summer.' None of the accommodation then was en-suite and the meals served to holi-daymakers were very basic by today's standards. Foreign travel was rare and the English diet was still influenced more by wartime rationing than continental cooking.

David remembers the growth of the holiday camps. They took much of the business from the guest houses, appealing as they did to the younger families. He supplied them, too, with catering equipment, staying with his employer for 43 years before retiring. 'I saw the holiday trade here change and then slowly die,' he mused. 'We could provide most things here except guaranteed sunshine. People started going to Spain. Who could really blame them?'

Having witnessed the decline of the local holiday business David was not sorry to retire. He still keeps in touch with his old employer and helps out now and again. His years of experience are still valuable to the firm; they didn't want to lose him completely.

With his wife, he has recently celebrated 50 years of marriage. Their son and grandchildren, together with their many friends in the town, organised a large party. It was unusual for David not to have been the organiser. This time he and his wife were evening's celebrities. Against a backdrop of massive change, both in the town and in society in general, David's job, wife and home have changed little. However he does not live in the past; he has taught himself to use a computer and enjoys keeping up with today's technology.

David does feel that today we are too inclined to feel sorry for ourselves and lean on others for support. Of course he recognises the benefits of the social support available to families today. 'In my day,' he recalled, 'each family had to look after itself. If you had a problem you sorted it; there was no-one you could turn to.'

David is philosophical about the future. 'We can only pass on what we have to the next generation,' he reflected. 'It is for them to decide how to use it', he concluded.

Expecting help

David was brought up in a time when the National Health Service, and Welfare State were political visions rather than realities. Having endured the deprivation of wartime England, sacrificing further education and career to care for an ailing parent seemed quite normal.

Critics of today's society condemn the way in which families expect their elderly to be cared for by the state. People no longer feel committed to looking after their parents when they become infirm. Instead they expect to be able to pick up the phone, call for assistance and have the problem taken away. But why do we see ageing parents as a problem anyway?

The perception that the weaker members of our community, be they old, frail or living with a debilitating health condition, are a burden on us is relatively new. The materialistic modern age encourages us to focus on personal gratification without distraction. That sense of duty to care for those around us which once was necessary is now considered intrusive.

Celebrating individuality

Sometimes people who choose not to conform are celebrated rather than rejected. Norwich over the past 20 years has had two fine examples.

For many years Marigold (as he was known) was one of the city landmarks. Tall, black and wearing bright green rubber gloves, he would stand beside the inner ring road directing the traffic.

Nobody knew where he came from but everybody knew when he was there. He brightened many people's journey to work, waving to them and all others in his bewildered attempt to help the traffic flow more smoothly. At times it was reputed he would be taken from the street and detained in a mental hospital. But nobody really knew.

Today 'puppet man', an elderly entertainer with the string puppets and music amplifier, performs his own very special song and dance routine in the Norwich Haymarket. Clearly at odds with the world in some way, his behaviour is unusual and considered by many to be entertaining. There is even a puppet man fan website. He has unwittingly become a tourist attraction in his own right.

It is likely that both Marigold and the puppet man live with a long-term mental health condition. That condition gives them the courage to be themselves and the resilience to ignore the occasional jibes from insensitive passers-by. Why can't we celebrate the individuality of everyone we encounter? We no longer feel the need to care for others but do need to rediscover the need to care about them.

Andy

Like David, Andy's earliest memories are of the Second World War. With his father and uncle away in the army his mother was left to care for the children alone. Night was spent in the Morrison shelter and he has memories of his mother forcing him to wear his gas mask during air raids.

The local newspaper contained names and photographs of those recently killed, which his mother would go through highlighting her childhood friends, now dead. It did not help that her brother, his uncle, was a prisoner of war in the Far East. He told me about a badly burned letter that eventually arrived to say that he was safe. The plane carrying the letter had been shot down. At the same time Andy was being bullied at school by his teacher to try to make him write right handed. Bullying continued at his senior school because he was not achieving academically, even the head-master told him he was lazy and a fool.

It is no surprise that today Andy campaigns against injustice and is a pacifist.

In common with most of us Andy grew up, got a job, got married and had children. In many ways he was just one of the crowd, a man you would pass in the street and hardly notice. Andy became unwell while a fireman after reacting to a prescribed drug. Andy had learnt his own coping skills whilst at school but both the now physical and mental damage became too much as he tried to care for his large family.

What followed for Andy was a 30-year journey through the mental health support system. A complicated pattern of symptoms led to varying diagnoses over the years. The general consensus was that he had manic depression. He also developed some physical illnesses which in time became debilitating in themselves.

He spent much time in hospital being fed various cocktails of drugs. Some he became addicted to and others were prescribed to deal with the side-effects of others. When feeling better in himself and keen to reduce his reliance on medication, he suffered withdrawal symptoms. These often led to spells in mental hospitals, where he shared wards with detoxing drug addicts from the street. In his forties he found out he was dyslexic and not able to work. He educated himself, achieving 7 'O' levels

Andy became an expert on the complicated biochemistry of antipsychotic drugs. He researched the subject widely and discovered to his horror that many of the drugs he had been given had well documented cases of unpleasant side-effects. Andy, through complaining about many of these debilitating effects, was considered by friends and family to be a hypochondriac.

That he was ill and needed treatment is not a point he disputes. What he does feel angry about now is that the drugs he was prescribed were often causing his ill health and that was not explained to him.

He told me about his first depot injection, given to stabilise him (or so he was told) so that he could go home from hospital. The injection was given and he was sent home for the day to see how he got on. The violent reaction his body had to the chemical terrified him and shocked his family.

He remains hurt that as his children were growing up they never really knew him. Instead they saw a shell emptied by pharmaceuticals. Their growing up time together can never be reclaimed

In the past few years he has won his battle with his illness. He no longer takes medication and no longer experiences the extreme symptoms that for so long damaged his life. He has researched the subject with the intellectual rigour you would expect of a PhD student. Reading his notes you wonder what he could have been in his career had mental ill-health not held him back.

Today he is a common sight around the city. He is one of those people you see whose face tells you that he has really lived. He says he hopes those people who gave him a wide berth perhaps fearing his illness now see him differently as he just gets on with his life - and his causes - his way.

True diversity

When historians look back on the 21st century Britain they will no doubt draw many conclusions from our current preoccupation with diversity and equality. Commentators say that we have defined minorities with such accuracy and enthusiasm that the majority are beginning to feel marginalised themselves. We are encouraged to value and celebrate diversity. But what does this really mean?

People like Andy are in many ways disadvantaged and marginalised by society. However, he is white, straight and can see hear and speak for himself. Very few of those politically-correct participant's screening forms that ask you to tick a box or two to describe yourself ethnically, sexually and in terms of your abilities would have a box that captured these problems. The more people seek to be inclusive, the more excluded those who do not fit into the convenient minority categories feel.

Another worrying symptom of this preoccupation with social inclusion was illustrated by a conversation I had recently with a serving policeman. He works in a large town that has a fast-growing European immigrant population. That immigrant population has developed its own infrastructure, with specialist shops and social groups to meet their needs. He told me without a hint of cynicism how good it was that we now had such a diverse community in his town.

I don't think he meant what he was saying. Surely in an ideal world we would not choose to highlight those who would differ from ourselves. Instead we would just accept them for what they are - people.

How well are you adapting to the changing world? Are you noticing how your attitudes are evolving? Here are some questions to help you decide:

Have you changed your views on a topic because someone you love sees things differently to you?

Think back to when you were a child. **How different were attitudes then towards people with different race, religion or sexual orientation? How have you changed over the years?**

We are all encouraged to be politically correct. But how much of what you say or do is matched by what you feel inside? **How can you become more real and true to yourself, so that you genuinely become more tolerant of people who see the world differently to you?**

Seven

Challenging

'The greatest challenge to any thinker is stating the problem in a way that will allow the solution.'

Bertrand Russell (1872 – 1970)

Challenging those around us, their attitudes, perceptions and beliefs is part of growing up. Even as a baby we push against the barriers of parental authority to see how far we can go.

Our first attempts at challenging authority are often self-defeating. As a small child you have little influence over anything except yourself. Refusing food, refusing to sleep or choosing to shit yourself rather than use of the potty are the main weapons in your battle for supremacy.

It is perhaps these early experiences of damaging ourselves to challenge those around us that lead to many of our problems later in life. The professionals tell us that suicide is often an expression of anger against someone else.

In fact self harm in all its forms remains one of our most potent weapons as we fight for individuality throughout life.

Challenging is also one way we bring about change in the world. Simply by questioning the way things are we bring them to people's attention. If no one had questioned why we do things the way we do we would probably still be living in caves.

The trouble is that in the world today most people are just too busy doing things to wonder why. It takes those who choose to live on the fringes of society to help us all to pause now and again to question what we are doing and why.

Writers and other artists, together with others who choose not to fit in, often choose to rise to the challenge of challenging us all. Art in all its forms provides an excellent metaphor with which to challenge our perceptions.

I recently spent an hour staring intently at some watercolours by Adolf Hitler. These had been embellished by Jake and Dinos Chapman to create challenging works of art. What struck me most was the fine delicate detail Hitler had created with his paintbrush to create tranquil landscape scenes. It suggested to me that there was more to the man than history would have us believe.

It seems to me that society endeavours to challenge those who challenge it. If your behaviour differs widely from what is considered normal you find yourself excluded for treatment. This has always been the case. I wonder how many of

those burned at the stake as witches were simply unfortu-
nate people tormented by the voices are heard in their
heads? Today they would have a very different diagnosis
and treatment.

Nick

Nick chose to study psychology and graduated with a degree
from Durham University last year. His mother is a hospital
radiographer and his father an IT manager, also working in
the NHS. In common with many young people Nick wanted
a career where he could make a difference in the world.

He wanted to work at the very coalface of mental health
and joined the team at the Norvic Clinic in Norwich. This is
a forensic psychiatric unit to
which people are referred
usually by the Courts. They come
here because their behaviour,
as a result of their mental ill
health, has caused them to
commit a crime.

The organisation's web-
site describes its clients as
'patients displaying significant behavioural problems
due to a current episode of
mental illness and requiring

treatment and management in a controlled environment'. in other words these are challenging people who may pose a threat to others as well as themselves. They are often very disturbed.

It is hard to work out why Nick has chosen to work in this environment. He tells me he enjoys working with people others would rather ignore. He clearly derives great satisfaction from helping somebody who arrives very disturbed to eventually leave in a much better condition.

At times his work is dangerous, particularly if someone becomes very unwell and violent. He has been trained in how to restrain people when they become a danger to themselves and others. The work is tough but clearly rewarding.

However challenging the people he works with become to Nick they remain people. He has the ability to see through their fear and distress to recognize the vulnerable human being hidden inside. 'The abnormal is feared,' he told me, 'by most people. Yet within every abnormal person, there is someone normal trying to be heard'.

Traditionally, people like this would have been sent to a secure hospital such as Rampton or Broadmoor. Places like the Norvic Clinic enable them to be treated closer to home so contact with family and friends is not totally lost.

Nick feels strongly that society is too quick to make judgements about those whose behaviour challenges convention. 'It's not their fault they have a mental illness,' he explained. 'You or I can choose how we behave, but when your illness makes you very, very disturbed, you're less able to make those choices.'

Challenging stigma

Stigma is natural, almost instinctive. We all tend to take the course of least resistance and follow the herd. If someone is obviously different from us, we tend to treat them differently. We choose to live, play, work and procreate with people who match our vision of how people should be. Those who seem different are shunned and avoided.

Stigma is best understood by those who have suffered it. They know what it feels like to be on the receiving end of other people's prejudices. Those prejudices are usually founded on fear or ignorance. People choose not to find out what life looks like from the other person's perspective. It is easier simply to avoid confronting both the people and what they represent to you.

Living Library

One really effective way that stigma can be challenged is by staging a living library. The concept was developed by a group of Danish youngsters in response to one of their friends being stabbed in the street on a Saturday night.

They created a movement called 'Stop the Violence' and quickly gained 30,000 supporters. At a large music festival they organised their first living library event to give people the chance to speak with those whom they might otherwise not understand.

One of those friends, Ronni Abergel, has introduced the living library to Great Britain. I was fortunate enough to be a "library book" for the day in Whitechapel. He gave me an opportunity to experience the living library for myself.

Each of the books, or more specifically each of the people acting as books, represented a particular topic or theme which many people have found difficult to understand. There were people from different ethnic groups, Vicky who lives with a condition called cherubism, which has disfigured her face, people who live with poor mental health and many others. I was there as a Bodyworlds body donor, having bequeathed my body to Dr Gunter Von Hagens to become a museum exhibit after my death.

Visitors to the library browse a catalogue and choose the person they want to speak to. They then have half an hour to converse with the person who represents a life challenge they would like to understand better.

I realised as the day went on that very few people have the opportunity to really confront their views and prejudices in such a direct way. Some of the best conversations will be reading the books themselves. In fact the room we called the bookshelf was alive with conversation.

The world needs more people like Ronni Abergel to create innovative and safe ways in which people can come together to understand each other better.

Poacher turned gamekeeper

Another way to gain an insight into the lives of others is to actually live your life the same way. Life for most people rarely stays the same. Our fortunes vary and at times we can be very happy and at others very sad. Stepping into someone else's shoes is a good way to see life from their perspective.

Try wearing old clothes for a day and selling copies of the Big Issue in your local high street and you will see how quickly other people's perceptions of you can change.

Sometimes illness, committing a crime or developing an addiction can take us into a whole new world. For some it is a one-way journey as they never recover from the setback. For others recovery leads to a new career helping others to make that same journey.

David

Despite what at first glance appears to have been an idyllic upbringing on a North Norfolk farm, David describes his childhood as dysfunctional. His father was a successful farmer but both he and David's mother suffered from depression. At the age of eight, he was sent away to boarding school where he experienced dysfunction of a more personal kind. He was sexually abused by older boys.

In his teens he submitted to peer pressure and started to drink and smoke. He was also introduced to drugs; hardly hedonism but more escapism. Adolescence saw his consumption of drink and drugs increase dramatically. 'I was part of a social set,' he said, 'where partying played a part in every weekend', he added. Young Farmers certainly used to live well, with some among their number well able to afford whatever opportunity came their way.

After graduating David returned to the family farm. He also became a volunteer at a local drug and alcohol support project. He was already in a long term relationship with his girlfriend, who also lived in Norfolk. They became engaged, started living together and for the first time he felt under control.

Then tragedy struck. His fiancée died in a car crash, alongside a friend, when on the way home from a day's shooting. David had bought her the car in which she died, trapped upside down in a pond. Evidence suggested that she had fought hard to escape, but to no avail. David was devastated and sought solace from drugs.

The darkest years of David's life drew to a close when he was arrested in possession of heroin. He was convicted, but also offered help. He had fled Norfolk after his fiancée's death but a return one day now seemed possible. First, though, he had to get clean and this meant eighteen months of rehab. Rehab he said was a 'tough time' with intensive counselling coinciding with being weaned off drugs and alcohol. He spent this time in a residential unit, from which there was little opportunity to escape.

This personal experience, coupled with his time volunteering back in Norfolk, led David to study psychotherapy. His own tragic tale, while unique to him, was similar to the knocks life deals to many. He came to know other people in rehab and was touched by the challenging journeys they were making. Farming was, perhaps, now simply one of those demons he'd purged from his past. The future lay in the world with which he had of late become very familiar.

David spent ten years working in various clinics and institutions as a qualified psychotherapist and counsellor. He worked with fallen celebrities and convicted criminals. All, he said, had similar feelings and emotions, once the damaged layers of perception and learned beliefs had been peeled back. 'In every case there has been some trauma,' he said, explaining that these could include bereavement, violence, abuse or bullying.

It is perhaps often the case that when we have healed we return to the place where the hurt happened. David had kept in touch with his parents and sisters but certainly had not been a frequent visitor to Norfolk. A combination of unhappy memories and a feeling he'd messed up here kept him away.

With time and treatment the pain had subsided. His new life, work and now a wife were elsewhere. Norfolk didn't seem as important any more.

By now with children of his own, David recognised that Norfolk was a great place to raise a family. Coast, country and city, all convenient, clean and safe; he felt ready to return and so he did. His parents are still alive and living here although he sees little of his former social circle. 'They have changed little over the years,' he explained, 'whilst I have changed so much.'

He now works in Norfolk as a psychotherapist helping people deal with their own demons. While in any professional client relationship he is unable to share his own past, he is confident he is well equipped to deal with whatever is revealed in his consulting room. He also works with a local mental health charity, where his clients are people who would be unable to afford his fees.

David knows, having worked with people from every walk of life, that we are all intrinsically the same. 'What makes us different, 'he explained, 'is the way life's experiences both good and bad shape our values, ideals and perceptions of ourselves and others.'

It has been said that it is our similarity to those around us that encourages us to be different. David would agree that while individuality is to be encouraged and prized, no one has the right to declare themselves better than others in any way. We need others to be different if we are to define ourselves.

Challenging the helper

David is qualified to help people deal with their problems. Not only is he fully trained to do this but he has also learned much from his own experiences. Not everybody who offers to help is as able as he is.

Of course volunteers have a very important part to play in keeping everything working. But sometimes the well-meaning helper can actually do more harm than good. This is a particular problem when the helper has a position of authority and so the vulnerable feel obliged to accept their offer of support.

Sarah

Sarah's childhood was dominated by the number of siblings she had. Her father was an academic and her mother fully occupied caring for Sarah and her ten brothers and sisters.

She told me how people in their neighbourhood made all kinds of assumptions about her family because it was so large: "People seemed to think that because we were many we were also stupid." The reality was different. Her parents had a large family because they wanted to, not because they did not know how to use contraceptives.

That said, Sarah's performance at school was not outstanding largely because of a growing feeling in her teenage years that there was no point in trying. Three of her brothers, on the other hand, have each achieved four A grade A levels and gone on to complete PhDs. Sarah was more sensitive to the jibes and jostling handed out to her by her peer group, who mocked her for being one of a large family.

She first became depressed in her mid teens and has struggled to maintain good mental health ever since. She doesn't blame the prejudice she experienced for her condition. However she is saddened by the fact that so many people judged her by her circumstances not by her personality or ability.

After university she trained as an occupational therapist. At her interview for her first hospital job she revealed that her mental health was not brilliant. She got the job and enjoyed working with people she could really help.

However, her career in the NHS came to an end after returning from time off with stress. She was told in no uncertain terms that it was not possible to be both an occupational therapist and a patient. Her health seemed to suggest that she was better suited to being a patient of the NHS than an employee. Fortunately that kind of attitude is fast disappearing.

Without the routine of a job her health deteriorated and it was 10 years before she worked again. Her biggest fear was that she would end up incarcerated within the mental health system, a scenario she described as "losing my life totally." In fact this did not happen, although Sarah did receive lots of different treatments as the psychiatrists tried to help her to recover.

At one point she attempted suicide. Life no longer seemed worth living and she walked into a wood near where she lived, climbed down into a ditch, took a massive Paracetamol overdose and waited to die. What changed her mind was when a group of young people almost discovered her hiding place when they came into the wood to play Frisbee.

I guess it was the contrast between the seriousness of her first suicide attempt and the light-heartedness of their game that brought home to her the fact that life was for living, not ending. She climbed out of the ditch and sought help.

A well-meaning friend at around this time introduced her to a local clergyman. The vicar in question had something of a reputation for his healing ministry and the friend thought he would be able to help.

In fact the friend was wrong. Sarah did not find it at all helpful to have the vicar attempting to exorcise her of the demons he was convinced had taken up residence within her. 'He would sit me down and shout loudly in my ear demanding that the demon got out of my body,' she told me. 'Being ill was bad enough,' she said with a wry smile, 'but this guy thinking I was possessed by the devil was not exactly helpful.'

Today Sarah is a writer. She has brought to her creative work the high and low points of her life to date. She runs a project that encourages people to talk about their experiences, which are recorded as living histories. There is no doubt that, having been on the receiving end of more than 40 attempted exorcisms, several programmes of ECT and a variety of drug regimes, Sarah understands how the well-intentioned can damage the individual.

One of many things that Sarah and I have in common is an interest in the views and experiences of older people. In my case this is arguably an attempt to reassure myself that I have lots to look forward to. In Sarah's, however, it is more a desire to help older people break down the misconceptions that younger folk hold about what it's like to be old.

Sarah's Housing Association flat is not in the most desirable part of town. You reach it by climbing the shared stairway where footsteps echo against the empty walls. Once inside it is actually rather pleasant with literature-lined walls and comfortable furniture.

In some ways her flat is a metaphor for her life. From the outside people have found it easy to dismiss her and underestimate her potential. Take the trouble to find your way in and you find a person rich in knowledge with a real sense of mission in the world. As Sarah herself summed it up, her poor mental health has liberated her to find her own way in life.

Challenging yourself

It is always difficult to challenge ourselves. Our attitudes and beliefs are engraved on our minds in ways that make it difficult to change. It is rather like a tombstone which has words and numbers carved into its surface. The only way to change the message is to remove the top layer of stone to create a fresh clean surface on which to carve.

Most of us find it easier to challenge other people than to challenge ourselves. If you can change the other person's attitude then of course you no longer need to change your own. And that is the problem with stigma.

Challenging yourself and being receptive to new ideas keeps you young, fresh thinking and potentially more popular than you otherwise might be. It can be a struggle to see things from other people's perspectives but in my experience it is always worth the effort.

A good way to challenge yourself is to take the trouble to look for the reality that sits behind the perception that faces you. When I was in my 30s people in their 50s appeared to be too old to really be in touch. They seemed to lack the enthusiasm or vigour I felt essential to making any kind of worthwhile contribution to the world. They were simply old people in the making.

Now I am in my 50s I find it hard to appreciate that people in their 30s are actually capable of all they seem to be undertaking. They certainly have the qualifications and skills but how can they possibly succeed with so little experience and such youth.

The challenge for me is to remember how I felt 20 years ago about people the age I am now. I now know that the perception I had then was wrong. Because I have judged older people in the past it makes it easier for me to appreciate how people even older than me might think.

How can you challenge your own perceptions about other people? Ask yourself, or discuss with friends:

How have you seen prejudices change in your life time? What do you think we accept today but will somehow reject in the future?

Could you work with challenging people as Nick and David do? If not, why not? What do you think you'd find most challenging?

Do you think before you speak? Have you ever found the opportunity to talk to someone who is an 'expert by experience' in something you feel strongly about? Would you attend a living library?

Eight

Making choices

' It is our choices . . . that show what we truly are, far more than our abilities.'

JK Rowling 1965 -

Some 15 years ago I did some consultancy work with a training company. The main focus of their work was to help people regain control of their lives. People from all kinds of backgrounds went through their training programme and came out the other side recognizing that they could make choices about how they spent their time.

The argument was that we all can choose the way we live, the company we keep and the work that we do. All one has to do is appreciate the implications of changes one might choose to make.

For example, just suppose you really dislike your job. You could give it up tomorrow. Everyone has the ability to resign and walk out. It would be easy to walk into your manager's office tomorrow and say that you are leaving and never coming back. But what are the implications of this action?

Without a job you cannot support your current lifestyle. The mortgage, car, holidays, nights out would all have to go and you would have to live a very simple life on a dramatically reduced income. But you *can* choose to do this; it really is up to you.

In other words if you want to maintain the lifestyle you must tolerate the job. If you want to give up the job you must compromise on lifestyle. But you have the choice and make the decision to go to work every Monday morning because you want what that work gives you.

The next challenge that the training company would introduce was to invite people to look objectively at the things they do because they feel they need to. For many people recognizing that they can downsize a little without really sacrificing much is enough. Just as few hate their job enough to resign tomorrow only a few people would really choose a minimalist lifestyle.

What is most important for all of us is that we actually make some choices. It is neither desirable nor really acceptable to just jog along, complaining about our lot. Doing something is always better than doing nothing.

Talib

Talib was born and raised in Jutland, the son of a career soldier in the German army. He had no strong ambitions at school, although from the age of six was keen on martial arts. His father was born during the Second World War and so Talib's grandparents were his only living link with that dark period in his country's history.

That said, Talib has strong views about the way his country continues to be castigated for what took place three generations ago. 'The Holocaust was not the first genocide in history nor was it the last,' he told me, 'yet even today the German people are constantly reminded of that shameful episode in their history.'

He became exposed to Eastern culture after his parents divorced when he was 13. His mother's new partner was Turkish and many visitors to the family house were now Moslem. He trained as a chef because, he says, 'I liked eating'. However he soon found that this career choice did nothing for his social life. Whenever his friends were playing, he was working.

It was at the age of 18, when he was relaxing in a Turkish tea house in Germany, that he really began to think about Islam. 'I loved the warmth and hospitality,' he told me, 'and from what I could see, they seemed to have a calmness about their lives that I wanted.' One thing led to another and, with the support and encouragement of the local Imam, he converted. It is customary when you embrace Islam to take a new name, relevant to your faith. Talib chose a new name with the same initial as his birth name.

Any doubts he had about becoming a Muslim disappeared when he first visited Mecca. 'I felt as if I'd come home,' he said, describing the tremendous feeling of belonging he'd experienced. He was just 20 at the time. When he returned to Germany, he was suddenly struck by the immodest way women dressed in Europe. 'I'd not noticed their nakedness before,' he told me.

During his 20s, Talib's faith strengthened. He married a German girl who had also discovered Islam and was running a language school in Germany. Life was good, but he knew there was more to be discovered. The couple became part of a religious community and travelled. In Sudan he learned to speak and read Arabic, gaining from that language a deeper understanding of Islam.

It was with this religious group that Talib first came to the UK. Initially they settled in Slough although later he and his wife moved to Norwich where they became members of the city's Muslim community.

Talib presents something of a prejudice paradox to the people who meet him. He is European and therefore does not conform to the popular image of a Muslim. He does have a beard and his wife covers her head in the traditional Muslim way. He has also chosen to substitute his birth name with one more in keeping with his faith.

The great thing about Talib is that he is very knowledge-able about all things Islamic. He welcomes the opportunity to help people see Islam in a more positive, non-threatening way. By being so open about his chosen faith he helps us to understand it much better.

Making up our own mind

One of the things that people do readily is to blame others for the situations they find themselves in. Placing the responsibility on someone else in some way absolves us from being responsible about decisions ourselves.

If you have children you will be familiar with this concept. Imagine your children are playing in the garden, you hear a crash and go outside to investigate. Your daughter has just thrown the ball and broken the window in your shed. It was clearly her as she is standing there looking horrified at the pile of broken glass.

You calmly ask her why she broke the window and she says immediately "because my brother made me." clearly her brother, who is three years younger and half her size, did not physically grapple with his sister, place the ball in her hand and help her throw it. What she means is that he challenged, goaded or somehow made her mad enough that she threw the ball herself.

When we grow up we blame our parents, siblings, employer, neighbours or anyone else we can think of for the things that we do. It is so much easier to follow the course of least resistance and blame others when we feel unable to follow our own path.

It is of course true that our parents influence our values and attitudes. As children we are very receptive to ideas and take what our parents say as fact. You could argue that Talib only became a Muslim because his mother introduced him to her new Muslim partner at an age when he was impressionable.

Part of growing up is rebelling against those parental values that have been instilled in us. Even if we return to them after a period of exploration it is still important to make our own choices about our lives.

Sometimes, however, rebelling against parental desire completely changes the direction our lives will travel. In more cases than not that turns out to be no bad thing!

Rob

Rob and his wife Linda have lived in Norfolk for 25 years. They originally came to be near to Linda's children who were living here with their father. 'We lived in Kent,' Rob explained, 'and it was too far away for Linda to be able to see as much of the children as she wanted.'

The couple's lives had been inextricably linked for many years. Rob was born in Kent and privately educated, but he left for South Africa as soon as he was able. 'I wanted to leave and put as many miles between my parents and myself as possible,' he said. 'I wanted to make my own way in the world rather than live out their plans for me.'

In South Africa he teamed up with some other young Brits and life was good. His girlfriend fell pregnant and they married, although unfortunately the relationship did not last. Linda, too, married another from that same group of friends and borrowed Rob's then ex-wife's redundant wedding ring for the ceremony.

Some time after Linda's marriage also ended and the group had all returned to England, Rob and Linda married; ironically once more that same ring was used.

When Rob came to Norfolk he bought some derelict farm buildings at the end of a narrow lane, surrounded by fields, miles from anywhere. He and Linda still live there today, with their son, Linda's daughter and her partner. Rob has extended the living accommodation to include more of the buildings as the need for more space has arisen. The result is a unique home that reflects the couple's desire to live in harmony with their surroundings.

'I've recently become fascinated by composting', Rob told me as he showed me round. 'It's something we do badly in this country, yet we could do so much more to make us self sufficient.' Behind his vegetable plot is a range of compost heaps, together with what looks rather like an earth closet toilet. Nothing here is wasted.

It's likely that Rob gained his interest in the alternative and sustainable along the journey home from South Africa. You or I might catch a plane, but Rob rode his motorbike. What's more he did not exactly take a direct route, sailing from Mombasa to Mumbai, and then riding up through Asia into Europe.

For a time, Rob worked as a teacher and then as a social worker. He found neither particularly rewarding and even a spell as resident manager of a unit for what he described as 'delinquent teenage girls' failed to inspire him to remain working in the public sector.

Rob chose instead to cultivate his interest in self sufficiency and the outdoor life. Since moving to Norfolk he has worked with his hands, initially renovating old buildings and more recently as a roofer and jobbing builder. He even spent a year or so as maintenance man at a convent.

'I have seen where materialism gets you,' commented Rob, 'and have chosen to work to live, rather than live to work.' Evidence of that work life balance cliché is regularly seen by Rob as he travels round repairing roofs. He describes how people seem to be both busy and unhappy, despite having expensive cars, expensive clothes and expensive homes. 'It seems the more they have the greater their discontent,' he exclaimed.

By way of illustration of this point Rob reached up and brought down a crumpled old tin from a shelf above his head. 'This is my lunch tin,' he told me, 'I've been using it for more than 20 years.' The tin was certainly battered and worn. The lid was dished and quite thick. Rob explained that the tin itself was heavy enough to put in a fire to heat the contents, while the lid served as his plate. It struck me that if someone invented a device that could store, cook and serve a meal, and be small enough to tuck into your rucksack, it would be very expensive. It would also, I suspected, last for nowhere near as long as the tin that Rob rescued from a building site and has used to carry and cook countless dinners over the last two decades.

Rob has learned over the years that there is more pleasure to be gained from well-used, familiar objects than from those newly purchased. His home is filled with treasured items he and Linda have collected or acquired. I put my coffee mug down on what was clearly a fairly old table, yet Rob quickly slipped a mat under it to protect the wood's surface. 'This table marks,' he said, 'sorry about that.'

As Rob and Linda have matured over their 25 years in Norfolk, so too has their home and the things they use within it.

Both are slim, fit and maintain their good health with hard outdoor work and a sensible diet. Everything within their home is similarly well cared for; nothing is broken and nor does anything look new. From their time in Africa, they have come to appreciate that the value of an object is not in its price, but its usefulness. Their lifestyle is the antithesis of bling.

Rob refused to give his definition of normal. He said there was no such thing as everyone is different. 'I enjoy living a simple life, 'he said, 'and suspect that in time more will come to share my view that materialism creates a hollow, empty shell. My life is full and very happy.'

Wabi Sabi

Rob's simple but very happy lifestyle reminded me of an ancient Zen philosophy called wabi sabi. It encourages you to value and treasure things which are worn by frequent use. It helps you to appreciate the relationship you have with the everyday objects around you.

To me wabi sabi is the opposite of bling. It is not about wanting more but about enjoying what you have. It is about living in the moment, accepting imperfection and the transient beauty of the natural world around us.

Rob's home and everything about it is peaceful, tranquil and in tune with its environment. It contrasts starkly with the gadget-packed home of the unhappy materialist. It illustrated to me the distance I still have to travel in learning to value and preserve what I have rather than constantly seeking out the new.

Following our instinct

Ambition evolves over time. A young boy may want to grow up to become an astronaut. When he starts to choose his GCSE subjects he might still be interested in science, but less inclined to aim at the stars. At university he might study physics. Then on graduating he has to find a job and this might be quite unconnected from the subject he studied.

My own career has changed dramatically over the past 30 years. It is fair to say that only in the last eight years did I really begin to understand what I really want to do with my life. Changing direction to follow your instinct is far from easy. Not only do you have to persuade those close to you that what you are doing is right, you also have to persuade yourself. You sometimes also have to discard the knowledge and skills you have acquired to learn something new.

Oz

Although raised and schooled in rural Suffolk, Oz chose to study in a university in a very different environment. He did not deliberately set out to find a rather deprived urban environment, but today is rather pleased that he did.

Sunderland is very different from Suffolk and Oz was somehow changed by the marked differences between the two communities. In fact the contrast between his pleasant and pastoral middle class childhood home and the desperate circumstances endured by people he met in the North East shaped him almost as much as his degree course.

A more pleasant discovery at university was the girl who became his wife. She too had moved there to study and she too was moved by the difference between life there and in the more affluent south. The couple stayed in Sunderland for a while after graduating and then moved around the UK for a year or so.

Highlight of his travels around the UK was a spell in Oxford, as music editor for one of the first online CD retailers. 'My job entailed listening to music and writing a full review of each CD. People read these before making a purchase; it was very rewarding.' As is often the way with small, niche businesses, the firm was taken over by a major retailer. Reviews became increasingly less valued and Oz realised it was time to move on.

The couple decided to move somewhere new and put down roots. Two locations appealed: the Norfolk coast and south Wales. Both had wonderful countryside, long sandy beaches and a nearby city with a thriving arts culture. Norfolk won by a narrow margin and the couple moved here and looked for work.

Initially Oz temped at Norwich Union. The money was good and he wanted to take his time to find the right job for the longer term. His wife found a teaching job at the local college and life settled down to a routine.

The place where they bought a house was nice enough; a hundred yards from the beach and convenient for the shops. Nearby, though, were some large communities of people coping with poor housing, high unemployment and social deprivation. These reminded Oz of Sunderland and it somehow bothered him that while life for him was fine, for many of his neighbours, life was a real struggle.

Then one day his wife cut a job out of the local paper. A local charity was seeking a youth worker to work with young people experiencing poor mental health. She was undecided about applying and the couple discussed the opportunity several times without reaching a decision. Oz found himself drawn to the job, even though he had no experience of the voluntary sector or of mental health.

Eventually Oz and not his wife applied for the job. His enthusiasm and willingness to listen more than compensated for his lack of relevant experience. With a part-time assistant he found himself providing encouragement and positive support to a very troubled group of youngsters.

Oz is bothered by the way society reacts to the young people he works with. Many are recovering from severe mental ill-health and do not need to be regarded with suspicion and mistrust. 'All that does is drive them further into the dark place they are trying to leave,' he told me.

Most of his clients are male. All are in their late teens or early twenties. They dress as young people do, hooded tops, t-shirts and jeans. Many have tattoos and body-piercings;

it's the fashion and a way of feeling you belong. One young man described how he wore his hood up because it made him feel safe when out on the streets. 'He lacks self esteem,' Oz explained, 'and feels less threatened by those around him from inside his hood.' The problem was, as Oz went on to tell me, that people he passed in the street misinterpreted his appearance as an aggressive stance. The opposite was in fact the case.

Challenging stereotypes is something Oz does. He feels angry that people can be so quick to make assumptions about the young people he works with. He has observed that most prejudice and preconception seems to rest with the older generation. Contemporaries of the young people's parents seemed to have the biggest problems seeing his clients as people facing problems, rather than simply as threats.

He found that skipping a generation made all the difference. A lady in her seventies worked with his clients as part of a creative writing project. She seemed easily able to regard them as people not problems. They too respected her maturity and responded to the non-judgemental attitude towards them. Together they wrote poetry and prose, even publishing an anthology of their work.

Oz is not sure where his career is going to take him next. He finds his work with young people intensely rewarding, nurturing their confidence and developing the life skills they have somehow never been able to learn. Despite being an English graduate with no social care qualification, he seems to sense what his clients need and achieves sometimes dramatic results. Clients grow in his care and move on to bigger and better things.

Increasingly schools, colleges and others working with young people seek his advice. Suicide is a frequent risk with this client group and getting it wrong can lead to tragedy. Oz has to make some tough decisions himself. Can he make the biggest difference working with clients, work he loves, or by sharing his experience of success with others. Of one thing he is certain. That is that he is doing something worthwhile that he enjoys.

Stereotypes

The opposing perceptions generated by a young man wearing a hooded top are challenging in themselves. You have just read an example where a youth wore his hood up to bolster his confidence. Passers by found this threatening and withdrew, increasing his feelings of isolation and rejection.

We all face similar challenges. With a global population of 6 billion it is very difficult to be an individual. We choose the clothes we wear and the style of hair to reflect the image we wish to project to the world. Inevitably we choose to copy what we have seen others do before.

What this means is that when people meet us they form a first impression based on our appearance which could be very misleading. We assume that someone who is scruffy has less money than someone more tidily dressed. We associate ponytails with creative men and brightly-coloured clothing and jewellery with creative women.

Ethnicity, budget and environment add another dimension. Yet we rarely take trouble to find out if we are making the right choice when deciding how to treat the person we have just met. Perception quite clearly is not reality yet too often we assume that it is.

What choices have you made in your life so far and what choices have you yet to make? Perhaps these questions will help you make those choices:

To what extent do you feel you are your parents' child? Do you feel reassured or irritated when you feel yourself acting as you think they would once have done? Have you rebelled enough yet?

It is very easy to blame others for making us the people we are today. **But what steps have you taken, or could you take to become the person that deep down you really want to be?**

If you look at the work you do, or, if you don't work, at how you spend your time, how satisfied you with this? **To what extent do you feel you are following your instinct, or are simply on a treadmill?**

Nine

Drive

'Your time is limited, so don't waste it living someone else's life.'

Steve Jobs 1955

There is never enough time to do everything you want to do. It feels at times to most of us that we are running to keep up like a hamster on a wheel. That feeling of always being behind can create stress which slows us down making the problem seem even worse.

Yet some people appear to find time to do the most amazing things. They have a family, a demanding job, a hectic social life and still find time for something unusual as well. Perhaps they volunteer in some way, or play in a band, or perhaps they have an all-consuming hobby like astronomy or even train spotting!

People with intense drive usually know where they are heading. They have a vision that they are trying to realise. To them that vision is very real and they can see very clearly the person they want to be. They also have a clear view of the world around them and know how they want to change it.

Finally, they have the confidence and self belief to think that it is possible. It is self doubt that holds most of us back. It is human nature not to want to be the first to try anything new. But sometimes having the courage to be the first is all it takes to lead a revolution.

When I decided I wanted to be a published author nothing was going to get in my way. I spent hours in book-shops scanning the shelves to see what was stocked in the genre I wanted to write in. I looked at publishers' websites to see who was publishing books similar to the ones I wanted to write. I also made a point of meeting authors and trying to understand what it was really like.

I was relentless, calculating and determined to see myself in print. Of course there is really nothing new and all I was going to be able to do was present existing material from my perspective, coloured with my experience, in my own way.

Through hard work, commitment and networking I planned and executed my campaign to get a first book published with a major publishing house. Having achieved this I then worked hard to build the right relationship with the commissioning editor I hoped would eventually commission work from me.

Now eight years later this book is the first that I have published myself. That is yet another challenge, one that launches my career in a new and interesting direction. Having achieved the goal of being published I now have the goal of being a publisher. As soon as one goal is achieved another appears from over the horizon. That is what makes me a driven person.

Small is beautiful

Often the scale of the outcome belies the amount of effort and drive needed to achieve it. Personal achievement is too often measured by the size of what has been achieved rather than the effort needed to make it happen.

A good example is this story of journalist Jean-Dominique Bauby who suffered a major stroke that left him with locked-in syndrome. His story is captured in the book "The Diving Bell and the Butterfly" which he dictated by blinking an eyelid. It was the only way he could communicate.

The book was made into a film which illustrated well the huge effort it took Bauby to make the tiniest advance in his battle to communicate with those around.

Fiona

Fiona lives with bipolar disorder. She says that she is blessed with its eccentricity and cursed with its despair. She describes how mental illness drains through every crack in her life. Fiona decided to climb Ben Nevis.

It was not a spur-of-the-moment thing although the decision to start walking was. Fiona saw a leaflet promoting a walking group called 'Discovery Quest' at her local doctor's surgery. To impress her brother as much as anything else she took a leaflet and made a phone call.

She went to the introductory meeting to see what it was all about it. She decided to take her best friend to see if she could persuade her to join her taking up his new hobby. The group was especially for people with mental health problems.

When she first met the group she discovered that the quest in question was to walk the 96 miles of the West Highland Way and then climb Ben Nevis. It sounded both romantic and impossible but she decided to give it a try.

The training was tough. Every Wednesday they would meet and take a walk. Those walks got longer until they were out all day taking a picnic lunch to keep them going. 'I respected my body on

walking days, it was working well and my spirit was bright.'
Fiona told me.

Six months later, hardly believing it was really hap-
pening, they all set off in a minibus for the long drive to
Scotland. Fiona described how nervous as she felt and how
undeserving of this opportunity to do something rather
special. Her brother was an eight marathon runner and this
was her way of competing with him.

The next few days for Fiona were amazing. Everything
was new, from sleeping under canvas to eating large fried
breakfasts, and in particular hills. All her training walks had
been on the flat terrain of Norfolk and in Scotland it was
hilly.

Most people would be daunted by these challenges but
Fiona literally took them in her stride. She described how
her legs ached and how well she slept at night.

Finally the day came when the Ben Nevis was to be
conquered. The team was told to wear one layer of clothing
and carry as little as possible in their rucksacks. Fiona ate
what was recommended for breakfast and they set off at
eight in the morning shaking with cold and apprehension.

Six hours later they were near the summit and surrounded by misty clouds that draped the mountainside. Then
suddenly they were there. Fiona described to me the incred-
ible feeling of achievement she felt. 'Whatever happens to us
now, for the rest of our lives, however isolated or depressed

our mental health may make us our experiences in life belong to before and after Ben Nevis. Nothing can take away from us the place we found in the team discovery quest.' Fiona proudly explained

Simple is good

Sometimes it can be good to strive to do less rather than more. As we all lead increasingly hectic, busy lives, finding time to value the simple things can be difficult.

Fiona drove herself to climb Ben Nevis. For her it was an important step along the path towards recovery, or at the least a greater feeling of being part of society rather than on its edge. Others simply want to do less because they are already aware that they are doing too much.

During her visit to Scotland Fiona and her fellow trekkers were driven along a remote glen and dropped off one by one to experience a few hours completely by themselves. When discussing their spell of isolation later all found the experience moving. When did you last take time out to sit on your own outside and to marvel at the beauty of the natural world?

In Norfolk we are fortunate to have many remote places. My favourite of all of these is Holkham beach. It is the place I go, whatever the weather, if I feel that life and all its challenges are becoming too much for me. A half hour brisk walk from the car park takes you to a deserted stretch of dune-backed beach where the rustling pines, distant tide, scudding clouds and acres of isolation remind you how big the world is and how insignificant the individual within it.

Sonia

Sonia was born just after the Second World War ended. Her father and step father were German Jews who came to Britain on one of the last 'kindertransports' from Germany. Many of her family perished in the Holocaust. Her mother was English and Catholic.

She was raised by foster parents and returning to her mother at the age of 13 was considered to be a problem. She was introduced to antipsychotic drugs which continued to be prescribed until she was about 50. She thinks now looking back that the drugs were for the benefit of the parents rather than herself. They certainly made her easier to live with!

She was told that she had a chemical imbalance in the brain and this was called manic depression. She was admitted to hospital many times and each time she was well enough to leave the staff cheerfully told her that she would soon be back. They told her that manic depression was something you had to live with and hospitalisation was inevitable from time to time.

At 50 she made the decision to come off the drugs. To the casual observer this is a very small and simple decision to make. To Sonia it was a major challenge, going against the advice she had received throughout her adult life. What she wanted was to make life simpler and break the cycle of severe depression and relative calm.

Her psychiatrist was less than supportive, telling her that she would embarrass her family, run up huge debts and probably commit suicide. It is true that many people with manic depression, or bipolar disorder as the politically correct call it today, do go on spending sprees when experiencing a period of elation. But this did not happen to Sonia.

She has now lived without medication for more than 10 years. She's considered by those who know her to be completely sane but slightly eccentric. And as she told me, she actually likes being considered a little eccentric. One of her grand-daughters went to the toy shop and bought her a bag of marbles. She proudly handed them to her saying, 'these are to replace the ones you've lost Nanny.'

Today you would describe Sonia as one of Norfolk's colourful people. She is creative and loves art. For a time in her life she was a teacher and she enjoys helping others see the world through her eyes. What Sonia has pushed to achieve is simplicity. She lives a happy life with her partner and family, including her much-loved grandchildren. She no longer takes medication and it is many years since she had a spell in hospital.

She told me that the only thing left from those days in hospital and various day centres is an addiction to tea, coffee and cigarettes.

Defining success

I rebelled against my father, who wanted me to follow in his footsteps and work for a bank. I could think of nothing worse than being in an office dealing with other people's money. I went to Agricultural College because I preferred the outdoor life and enjoyed working on the land.

My father was disappointed by my career choice although that was forgotten when my younger brother left school and joined Barclays Bank. (In fact he did not stay there long!)

Unfortunately my father died when I was 25 years old. I did not have the opportunity to prove to him that my career choice was the right one for me. He would, I am sure, have been impressed if not proud of the fact that I spent many years starting and building my own businesses before focusing on my third career as an author.

The drive to do the things with our lives that our instincts and hearts tell us are the right things to do is very powerful. Understandably parents do not always value or really appreciate the choices we are making. In fact they can feel hurt that having made sacrifices themselves to raise us, we choose to follow a different path from the one they expected.

Jack

Youngest of four very bright children Jack graduated from Cambridge University a few years ago with a 'double first'. Determined to find his own way in the world he chose not to apply for any of the highly paid graduate entry schemes promoted to him in his final year at university. Instead he started his own business.

Ambition for Jack, however, was more about making a difference than making a mint. Balance this with his parents' decision to make whatever sacrifices were necessary to fund private education for their kids and you begin to see the dilemma.

Jack says his parents did a good job of keeping to themselves the inevitable worries that meeting an ever growing mountain of school fees created. Jack was not denied emotional nurture at any time, despite the ease with which his parents could have grown to resent the strictures imposed by their determination to give their children a better start in life than they had enjoyed themselves.

At school, although very talented, Jack soon realised that whereas for many of his peer group money was readily available finances in his family were somewhat tighter. He didn't go without but says he really appreciated the opportunity he had been given, that his wealthier peers seemed to take very much for granted.

Socially, he realised at an early age just how easy it was to feel inferior, simply because you had access to less money than those you were mixing with. His parents dreaded the 'where are you going for the summer,' questions so often asked at school gatherings. These are, of course, simply the ways people create a social hierarchy, albeit based on disposable income, rather than intelligence, social conscience or the positive impact you have on the lives of those around you.

After A level success in French, Maths, Latin and Politics, he could have chosen a number of degree courses. Perhaps increasingly aware that people are what matter, rather than things, he chose a Psychology, Politics, Sociology Tripos and loved every minute of his time at Cambridge. Predictably perhaps, he chose one of the less pretentious Colleges for his studies, choosing one preferred by less affluent, free thinking undergraduates.

That said, Jack did not grow up with a chip on his shoulder nor did he ever challenge his parents' considerable sacrifice. The youngest of four children, the path he trod to private education had already been trodden by his brother and sisters. He had the brain to benefit from the education and that for him was enough.

He describes himself as a dealmaker. 'You have to find win:wins when you've not got a lot to spend,' he told me. Unusually for one so young, he is also very introspective. 'It's only when you stop to see where you've got to, that you realise how last year's wild ambition has slipped into being a reality almost unnoticed,' he added.

He has also realised that wisdom is not necessarily the product of age and experience: 'Just because someone is twenty years older doesn't actually mean they know any more.'

He has learned to tread the fine line between rightfully respecting someone's age, without deferring to them because they are automatically any better than he is. 'It's just not true,' he said, 'that older always means wiser.'

Jack has worked hard on his self esteem and has enough successes under his belt to be quietly confident in his abilities. He also knows the importance of setting priorities and claims only to take on something new when he knows he can drop something less important to make the time.

In common with many bright people, he observes and learns from those around him. Asked who his champions are he produces a list. Each individual on that list has taught him something he values, although they may not have realised it at the time. Top of the page is his late grandfather, who was poorly educated and widely read. 'Granddad educated himself,' he said, 'proving that you don't have to wait for others to teach you.'

Other major influences on his life have included the family of his first long-term girlfriend. He lost his innocence there in more ways than one, gaining first-hand a valuable insight into how another family dealt with life, work and, inevitably, money. He has also studied those American motivational speakers, even travelling to the US to hear them first-hand. When Jack sees something he wants, he goes all out to get it; he is admirably ambitious.

His own business is very much a commercial retrospect of his life thus far. Recognising the difficulties he encountered as he grew up, privileged in so many ways, yet financially constrained, he now works with young people as they make those same intellectual connections and career choices. By helping others over the hurdles he himself has so recently crossed he feels able to build their confidence and accelerate their careers.

Norfolk may not keep Jack though. He already spends a lot of time in London and realises that this is where those with real influence are to be found. 'I love Norfolk and everything about it,' he said by way of conclusion, 'but the fact remains that if you want to get on, you almost always have to get out.'

What are you driving at?

Communicating with others about what we are driven to do, and why, is a challenge in itself. Having a clear vision and sense of purpose is one thing but sharing it with others can be difficult.

At some point Jack would have had to explain to his parents that his vision for his future did not involve a high-flying city career. He would have had to explain to them that his ambition was to make the difference rather than a mountain of cash.

Getting the point across, or rather failing to, is one of the things that leads to stigma and prejudice. Because people live such different lives assumptions are made about what others may or may not know. For example a manager asking a Jewish employee to work on a Saturday may not understand why the answer to the question will almost inevitably be no. The fact that Jewish tradition demands that you do not work on Saturday may not be understood. Resentment can grow leading to other problems.

The question the manager may never ask is 'would you be prepared to work on Sunday.' This is because the manager has probably been brought up to regard Sunday as a day of rest. If a practising Christian it will be a day when work is not done. To his Jewish employee Sunday is a day when he is very likely to be happy and willing to work overtime.

The entrepreneur is taught to develop what is called an elevator pitch. They are encouraged to imagine that they are in a lift in a tall building with the person they would most like to recruit as either customer or investor in business. They have until the doors open on the 15th floor to get their message across and to interest their fellow passenger enough to commit to further dialogue.

The formula that many use to get the message across quickly and simply is this: they say who they are, what they do, what they are looking for and how this benefits the other person. Speed networking is becoming popular in the business world. It presents an ideal opportunity for the entrepreneur to practise that elevator pitch.

Wouldn't the world be a friendlier place if everybody could say what was driving them and why in a simple 90 second pitch?

What drives you to live your life the way you do? How well do you explain your motivation to those around you? How can you help the people you love to develop a clearer vision for their lives? These questions might help you:

What are the three big things you want to achieve in the next three years?

How do you think the people close to you will respond to these ambitions when you share them?

Try to prepare your own elevator pitch that communicates quickly and simply what you hope to do and how that will benefit others. Good luck!

Ten

Learning from others

'Human beings, who are almost unique in having the ability to learn from the experience of others, are also remarkable for their apparent disinclination to do so.'

Douglas Adams 1952 - 2001

When we are born we know nothing. We look and listen and try to make sense of the world in which we find ourselves. We know when we are hungry, thirsty, wet or frightened. Everything else we learn.

And we learn from our parents because for the first few years of our lives they are the only people with whom we really have close contact. Our attitudes, perceptions and prejudices are instilled in us unwittingly by our parents.

They usually mean well and pass on to us impressions of the world as they see it. They in turn have picked up their perspective from their own parents and so on. That is why culture is so important and remains so alive, even today.

It is sobering to realise that in the space of 1,000 years there are only 40 generations to pass down and keep alive both traditions and expectations. That is why we still shake hands when we meet (to show that we are unarmed) and why we still recite nursery rhymes centuries after the meaning of the words has been forgotten. (Ring a ring of roses describes the symptoms of the plague that swept Britain in 1665).

The poet Philip Larkin captured parenting in one sentence: 'They fuck you up, your mum and dad. They may not mean to, but they do.' Our parents fill our heads with the very best of intentions. In adolescence we challenge our parents and in adulthood blame our mother and father for programming us in a way which is patently out of date.

Repeating history

It could be argued that one sign of maturity is a willingness to consider and possibly value history. Men and women have always been the same for thousands of years. Our emotional and physical selves are the same today as those of our ancestors thousands of years ago.

What changes is the context within which we live our lives. My grandfather grew much of his food on an allotment. Most of my food is collected from the supermarket. Our diets and tastes will have little in common but the feeling of hunger, or post-meal contentment, will be the same.

A good way to make sense of right now is to view today's challenges against the context of yesterday's world. The knowledge that the mentally ill were once put to death, then confined, then more recently subdued with powerful drugs makes it easier to understand the treatment regimes we see today. Care in the community is not a wild stab in the dark, more it is the next logical step in a continuum from exclusion to inclusion.

For some people studying history and the work of those who have gone before gives them real opportunity. They find themselves able to recover and recycle convenient and worthwhile formulae for success from the past.

Alan

Alan was born at Farnborough where his father was in the RAF. He grew up with airplanes and has maintained a lifelong fascination with them. As a boy he was more interested in how things worked than school subjects. He failed his 11+ much to the dismay of his father. That said, he did well at Secondary Modern School, finishing his time there as Head Boy.

Adolescence was a turbulent time. Alan was a moody boy, keen on planes and comics. Everything else frustrated him and he developed a fiery temper. It was his older sister's boyfriend who sat him down one day after he'd stormed out of the house in a rage. This young man was training for Christian ministry and listened to Alan as he struggled to express his feelings of anger and frustration.

That conversation sparked an interest in religion and Alan started reading the Bible. Before then he had only read comics. 'Anything with pictures,' was how he put it. The Bible both captured his imagination and helped him make sense of where he was in life and the world. He became a Christian - an act which further troubled his father, an atheist.

After school came an apprenticeship at Farnborough. He trained as an electro-mechanical engineer. At the RAF Institute of Aviation Medicine, he combined science with psychology to work in the area of ergonomics. 'Planes were getting faster,' he told me,' and pilots needed information more rapidly than the traditional dials and controls could deliver them.' Alan was part of the team that developed the head-up displays that project data into the pilot's field of vision.

His Christian faith continued to grow. He described how many physicists became clergy, their science helping them understand the order of nature and God's role in creating it.

Classicists, on the other hand, were often unsure as they often lacked the logic on which a scientist's faith is grounded.

Colleagues encouraged him to try for a university place and he did this, studying philosophy, history and psychology at Bangor. In his final year, he married a Welsh girl he'd been courting there.

After graduation he was ordained into the Congregational Church and became a minister in Northampton. The work was challenging as his church was in a poor neighbourhood. People needed to work before they could pray. He continued to study and researched the life of Philip Doddridge, an 18th century evangelist and scientist. He was awarded a Master's degree for the resulting thesis. He moved to another church in the industrial North East but regretted the move. He left the church and taught RE and Technical Drawing in a local school.

He continued to preach, travelling around the country at weekends in a tradition stretching back to the time of Wesley. A friend invited him to preach at a Baptist chapel in a rural Norfolk village. The pastor there had recently died and the congregation were hoping to appoint someone new. That person turned out to be Alan.

The congregation was small, as was the stipend. The manse, however, was an idyllic old house next to the chapel, with a huge garden and views over open fields. Both Alan and his wife had been raised in the country. Here was the place they could give their children that same outdoor upbringing.

Ministry here was very much a family affair, with both Alan and his wife actively involved in their growing community. Money was scarce and initially Alan taught at a local High School. Education funding cut-backs, however, meant that his time at school was relatively short; just two years.

There was, however, plenty to do within the village, ministering to his congregants and encouraging more people from the surrounding area to discover for themselves the joy that Christian faith had given Alan and his wife. Never materialists, the couple cultivated the large garden and patronised charity shops. Alan's engineering background proved invaluable as over their twenty years at the manse, he nursed four successive Morris Oxfords along. As each reached the end of the road it was used as a source of spare parts for its successor.

This life of devotion and material simplicity enabled Alan to continue to study theology. He embarked on a PhD, his research combining history, philosophy and religion. This was published by the Oxford University Press in 1990. He became increasingly interested in the Calvinists, who had fled oppression in France and the Low Countries to settle in Norwich. They had brought to the city a fundamentalist style of Christianity he increasingly found matched his own ideals and beliefs.

His faith evolved and it became clear that to be true to himself he should leave the Baptist church and strike out on his own. Others encouraged him to follow his instinct and, with some sadness, he left the village church to make a fresh start in the city.

The new church meets in a community centre, although much of the work is of an outreach nature. There is a city centre Saturday bookstall, selling a wide range of relevant publications, including books and pamphlets that Alan has published himself. He pointed out the startling fact that his Calvinist predecessors in Norwich had been the first to print a book in the city. They had imported a press from the Netherlands back in 1567.

Alan is in many ways a lone voice in Norfolk. Many consider it uncool to be Christian and many find his outspoken views on Islam, pre-marital sex and homosexuality at odds with contemporary 'PC' thinking. Without him, however, those views would perhaps never be voiced and we all surely benefit from being drawn into the debate. Theologically and historically, Alan's arguments are robust, fundamental and difficult to dismiss out of hand. It is his courage in his convictions that keeps him going, even though he has reached an age when many men choose to retire and slow down.

Alan's work is a lifetime's work and his good health and his determined nature means he will remain vocal on often thorny issues for many years to come.

Skipping generations

My own children are now adult and poised to embark on their respective careers. With almost the same inevitability that night follows day romance will increasingly feature in their lives. This means that at some time in the next few years it is likely that I will become a grandparent.

Philip Larkin never wrote about grandparents and the relationship they have with their children's children. However as I move towards that stage of my life I am becoming increasingly aware just how important good grandparenting can be. There is no doubt in my mind that grandparents have a special role to play, perhaps gently tempering some of the parental teaching the new generation will experience.

Mental health worker Oz, introduced in an earlier chapter, has found it possible to stimulate tremendous creativity in young people when helped by somebody old enough to be a grandmother. It seems that, whilst rebelling against people of their parents' age is inevitable, people who seem unbelievably old are by comparison listened to and their words taken seriously.

Jacob

Jacob is a young man about to go to university. His mother is one of five sisters born to a couple who did not have a son. Jacob and his mother's father had a unique relationship which both cherish and others admire.

The older man is now in his late 70s and determined never to retire. He left a regular employment in midlife, with a young family and a determination to succeed. In fact determination is the only word which can accurately describe what drives the man to do so much.

He started a business in a sector that was completely new to him and made a lot of money. At an age when most men are thinking of retiring he took up painting. However he did not just paint for pleasure. He has marketed postcards, framed prints and address books bearing his work to raise money for a charity he had started.

Being the first grandson Jacob always had a special place in the old man's eye. As a schoolboy he encouraged him to be enterprising by paying him to do odd jobs for his company. A strong bond of mutual respect grew between them and as Jacob matured so did a business partnership.

Having learned from his grandfather that determination can get you anywhere Jacob set out to market his grandfather's paintings around the world. He started with exhibitions in Norwich. Eventually he managed to persuade a leading New York gallery to host an exhibition in the USA.

Jacob was also very good at generating publicity. He knew, having seen his grandfather do it, how to push just hard enough to get the result he wanted from a journalist. The combination of publicity and promotion together set a course with the talent his grandfather clearly has as an artist.

They set up their business together when Jacob went to college and it clearly provided an excellent opportunity for his grandfather to teach him much of what he knew. It is perhaps no surprise that Jacob finished his business studies course with an exceptionally high mark.

Explaining how important his grandfather has been Jacob said; 'as soon as I got to know Granddad I always had a big ambition to make sure he knew that I would be a success in business and make him proud.' When asked what the three biggest lessons he had learned from his grandfather

Jacob said; 'first never give up; second always look for new ideas and finally get paid first!'

Moving on
Another thing we learn from other people is when it's good to move on. There is nothing worse than trying to swim against an irreversible tide of change. Yet sometimes we dig our heels in, deny that things are different now and fight a battle we can in no way win.

Those changes can be in ourselves as well as all around us. For example you might do a job of work for a few years and become bored with it. You look for a new challenge because you are ready now for the next step. Somebody else who has yet to experience the job you are leaving welcomes the opportunity to step into your shoes and take your place.

What almost always proves to be unsatisfactory is going back to where you started. It is really difficult to do the same thing all over again with any real enthusiasm. This is often as true of relationships as it of a job. When you've made the decision to move there can be no turning back.

Kim
Born in Wiltshire, Kim spent the first nine years of her life living with her grandmother on the Antrim coast. She later went to school in Swindon.

Her teens arrived at the same time as the three day week. The Government was struggling to control inflation and capped pay rises. This caused massive union dissent and for a time in 1974 domestic electricity supplies were regularly turned off. Kim often used the power cuts as her reason for not finishing her homework; the truth was she couldn't see the point in it.

She left school as soon as she could and joined the clerical team of a locally headquartered multinational. Although not academic, Kim was enterprising. At the age of 19 she bought her first house and took in lodgers to cover the cost of the mortgage. Although at the time she didn't realise it, this was to be a foretaste of what was to come.

She enjoyed work and also married in her early twenties. Life was good, but not for long. Her mother contracted cancer and the couple moved to Wiltshire to be closer to her. After five long years of illness, Kim's mother died at the age of 46.

Kim only realised recently that she has now outlived her mother. It was a shock to realise how young her mother must have felt; cheated out of perhaps another thirty years of life. 'I'm afraid it makes me rather cynical at funerals,' she told me. 'Why do people wail and beat their chests when someone dies in their nineties? They should accept that death is inevitable and rejoice that their loved one lived so long.'

Kim's marriage ended in divorce and she concentrated on work and her two children. It was a tough spell with little money to spare for luxuries. However she had stayed in property and so at least had a house.

She had a wide circle of friends and by chance accompanied one to a spiritualist meeting. She didn't believe in it herself, but her friend, recently bereaved, found the meetings comforting and wanted Kim there to hold her hand. 'I was the one non-believer in the room and the medium came to me straight away. She said I would soon be living under Nelson's column. I had no desire to live in London so dismissed it as utter rubbish.'

At about this time she took a fancy to her younger, and very attractive postman, and invited him out for a drink. They'd chatted when they bumped into each other in the local supermarket, and she felt that the attraction was mutual. He too was divorced and after a cautious courtship they moved in together. They decided to move from the South and run a business of their own at the seaside. A fresh start seemed the right way to mark this new relationship.

This romantic notion led them to Norfolk where they purchased a run down bed & breakfast guest house. Kim saw the potential and a deal was struck. In many ways it took her back to her first house where she had taken in lodgers to make ends meet. It was only later that she noticed Nelson's Column towering over the terrace of houses at the end of the road. She remembered the medium's prediction. It was, she admits, 'an amazing coincidence.'

The couple worked hard and the business became both select and successful. 'We didn't want to be cheap,' she said, 'so decided to be worth every penny of what we decided to charge.' That gambit worked and within a few years they were winning awards, as well as enjoying higher occupancy levels than most of their more traditional B&B rivals.

As with many seaside towns, a few well-established people rule the roost. These local grandees prospered in the heyday of the British seaside holiday when everyone went to the coast for their annual break. Today, the market is very different, but Kim feels frustrated that people don't try harder to reinvent their businesses, their town and perhaps even themselves. 'The council have invested in nice paving, seats and lighting,' Kim complained, 'but that alone won't bring business to the town. All they're doing is papering over the cracks,' she suggested.

Kim has decided to leave and, when you read this, will be happily settled in her new hotel in the French Midi. She'd visited France as a child and liked the place and speaks reasonable French. Her partner and children are looking forward to making a new life abroad. There seems little point in staying in Norfolk.

'We thought about buying a bigger place in this town,' Kim explained, 'but the business we looked at concentrated on accommodating coach parties. You can't provide quality food or good service when you're being screwed down on price by coach holiday operators.' Perhaps rightly, she decided not to head down-market and France seemed an obvious alternative.

The couple's Norfolk guest house had a national reputation and quickly sold. The buyers were a couple seeking a change of lifestyle and a business that needed no work to bring it up to scratch. They have bought a good business, but as Kim wryly pointed out, 'when you're at the top, there's only one way you can go.'

The French hotel is pretty run-down so Kim and her partner have to start again from scratch. It's less than an hour from the airport, which is served by a budget airline based at Stansted. Her first target market is the French. 'I want to win the support of the locals first,' she explained, 'we don't want to be a British hotel in France, more a French hotel with international customers.' It could be said that Norfolk's loss is France's gain.

Stretching yourself

For Kim a new challenge was to do what she had done before but on a larger scale and in a new place. It is an example of how a career as an entrepreneur can mirror a career in a large organisation. The skills acquired in one situation, once proven and polished, can then put to good effect in something bigger.

If we don't stretch ourselves we become complacent. That is true of almost every aspect of life. In our relationship with ourselves, our work, family and friends we have to constantly look for new opportunities or risk taking what we had for granted.

This also applies in our attitudes to those we encounter in our day to day life. The challenge here, however, is not to enrich an existing relationship but to create a better understanding. You can go for years standing at the same bus stop as someone else and never speak to them. You stand in the queue, are aware of each other, but are perhaps afraid to open a conversation. If you gain nothing else reading this book I urge you to try engaging with people around you in conversation.

Of course I am not an encouraging you to put yourself at risk by approaching complete strangers in dark alleys in the dead of night. It is more a case of breaking the habit of ignoring the people you see every day and trying to find out a little bit about them and their lives. Think about the bus queue, or whatever the equivalent might be in your day-to-day life, and start a conversation with somebody you recognize but do not yet know.

There are techniques that can help you break down the barriers and gain the confidence to be proactive rather than reactive as you seek to understand others. These include the living library described earlier in this book. Better known are speed dating and speed networking, both good ways to strike up a conversation in a safe environment where the rules are predetermined and there is no risk.

Above all else the biggest challenge in all of this is to open your mind, open your ears, open your mouth and come to discover the amazing wealth of talent, knowledge and experience that surrounds you within the community in which you live.

As you have read through this book and begun to see the new people you meet differently you, like me, will soon be saying many times, 'I know someone like that.'

By the same author:

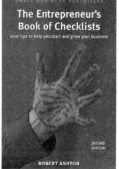

Achieving Business Alchemy - Hodder & Stoughton Aug 2002

Copywriting in a Week - Hodder & Stoughton Nov 2003

How to Sell – Hamlyn Aug 2004

The Entrepreneur's Book of Checklists - Prentice Hall Oct 2004

The Life Plan - Prentice Hall Nov 2006

Teach Yourself – Life at 50 for Men' - Hodder & Stoughton Jan 2007

The Entrepreneur's Book of Checklists 2nd Ed - Prentice Hall Aug 2007

Instant Entrepreneur - Prentice Hall 2008

Robert Ashton is an author, speaker and social activist. He has already written six books and seen his work translated into 13 languages.

As well as writing, Robert works with individuals and organisations seeking to become more entrepreneurial. All welcome his very practical, effective approach to enterprise. He particularly enjoys working with charities seeking to become more financially self sufficient.

Robert is a Trustee of Norfolk Community Foundation and Chairs a regional group for mental health charity Rethink. He is also a Governor of Norfolk & Waveney Mental Health Trust.

He lives with his wife Belinda in a converted barn in South Norfolk. The couple have two grown up children.

www.robertashton.co.uk

Profits from the sale of this book are being donated to the Stuff Stigma campaign, set up to challenge stigma in Norwich. www.stuffstigma.org